Minnesota
HOCKEY GREATS

Minnesota
HOCKEY GREATS

HOMEGROWN TALENT IN THE NHL

JEFF OLSON

FOREWORD BY LOU NANNE

THE
History
PRESS

Published by The History Press
Charleston, SC
www.historypress.com

Front cover, clockwise from top left: Imperial Oil-Turofsky/Hockey Hall of Fame;
Paul Bereswill / Hockey Hall of Fame; Wikimedia Commons; Lorie Shaull,
Creative Commons License (https://creativecommons.org/licenses/
by/2.0/); Michael Miller, Wikimedia Commons.
Back cover: Wikimedia Commons.

First published 2022

Manufactured in the United States

ISBN 9781467150958

Library of Congress Control Number: 2022936621

Notice: The information in this book is true and complete to the best of our
knowledge. It is offered without guarantee on the part of the author or The
History Press. The author and The History Press disclaim all liability in
connection with the use of this book.

CONTENTS

AUTHOR'S NOTE

I am very grateful to Sue Olson, my wife, for her very rock-solid support; to Lou Nanne, the "Grand Master of Minnesota Hockey," for supporting the original idea of a book to recognize and celebrate homegrown NHL greats, for his fantastic descriptions of some of the players and for his wonderful foreword; and to John Rodrigue, my editor, for his tireless work.

I am especially grateful for the descriptions of players by Lou Nanne. It was a thrill to work with Lou, an incredible hockey mind with a wealth of experience, in describing some of the players' skills and styles. John Rodrigue had many wonderful writing edits, for which I am very grateful. An additional wonderful experience in writing the book was to talk with a number of really fantastic people, such as Coach Scotty Bowman, Reed Larson and Phil Housley. Thank you all.

It was pure joy and fun to write about and describe the incredible achievements of Minnesota homegrown players. All Minnesotans can celebrate and are part of these stories of your neighbors or those across town or across the state. Hockey people at all levels are some of the greatest people on earth. It was an honor to write about this wonderful game and the extraordinary people who have made the game great. This is especially true of high school hockey coaches.

My special thanks go to people who gave extra fuel to my love of hockey. Coach Blatherwick, my high school hockey coach, for his passion and inspiration. Joe Zywiec, a master high school coach and an elite hockey mind, for the opportunity to coach with him. "Gundy," Coach Gunderson, college hockey coach, for his sheer joyful spirit of hockey and of life with lessons on how to live and for the chance to coach with him and know him as a friend. My father and mother, Howard Olson and Bettye Olson, for joining me in cheering on the spirit of this great sport. To all of these, and many more, I offer gratitude for your direction and support. Onward to more hockey! Lastly, many thanks to two great book lovers and grand literary minds, Ellen and Jim Hancock, for their literary guidance and support. Bravo!

In researching and writing the book, I was surprised to learn a number of things. First, is how many Minnesota greats came from areas close to one another. Second, is the magnitude of the changes and transformations for hockey in Minnesota during the twenty-two years from 1960 to 1982, the "Golden Era." Third, is the quality of high school coaches during the Golden Era and thereafter. Fourth, is the prominence of Coach Scotty Bowman with a number of players in the era. Fifth, is the strength of play of several players in the earlier era, such as Hall of Famer, Frank Brimsek and Cully Dahlstrom. Sixth, are the NHL accomplishments of players from states other than Minnesota, such as Massachusetts, Michigan, New York and Pennsylvania.

A TOUCH, A FEEL, A VISION, A SPECIAL SEASON

T he tip of his right index finger moved across the surface. He could feel an engraved line, then another line ninety degrees to that. It was an uppercase "L" on a silver surface like that of a chalice. He had thrown his hockey gloves off in the celebration at the end of the game. Then he felt the next letter, lowercase, and the next, and the next and so on. There it was: his name, *Langevin*, engraved on the Stanley Cup for the 1982 NHL champions, the New York Islanders.

Here he was, Dave Langevin, on Tuesday, May 17, 1983, now about 10:35 p.m., standing in his blue, orange and white number 26 Islanders jersey on the ice of the Nassau County Coliseum on Long Island in Uniondale, New York. Langevin was an integral member of this remarkable, history-making Islanders team that minutes before had won the series, four games to none, to become the 1983 Stanley Cup champions, beating the Edmonton Oilers, led by Wayne Gretzky, Mark Messier, Jari Kurri and Glenn Anderson. Now his name would be engraved for the fourth time on the Stanley Cup.

Dave could feel it. He could feel it in the game, playing this extraordinary game of hockey. He could feel it handling the puck with the blade of his stick, with his breakout passes to get out of the defensive zone, with leading the rush. He could feel it in his legs as he skated up ice from next to his goalie in his defensive zone.

Langevin had a steady journey of progress in hockey excellence, from his very first year in youth hockey on the neighborhood rinks of the east side of St. Paul, to the next step, then the next step, with ever-improving skating,

The Stanley Cup. Some of Minnesota's best have won the title. Dave Langevin (Hill-Murray, 1972) won four Stanley Cups with the Islanders. Bill Nyrop (Edina, 1970) won three Cups with the Canadiens. And Matt Cullen (Moorhead, 1995) won three Stanley Cups with the Hurricanes and Penguins. *Wikimedia Commons.*

shooting, passing and checking skills, and, probably his best skill: his hockey IQ.

Langevin stood between the face-off circles in the defensive zone in front of the goal when Billy Smith handed him the Stanley Cup. Smith, the MVP of the series, had shut out the "Great One," Gretzky, and the high-flying offense of the Oilers in Game 1 of the series, 2–0. Then the Islanders swept the Oilers in four games. Immediately after the fourth game ended, John Ziegler, the president of the NHL, presented the Stanley Cup to the Islanders and Coach Al Arbour and General Manager Brian Torrey. Ziegler handed the Cup to Captain Denis Potvin. Sporting a black Fu Manchu moustache, Potvin, a big, smooth-skating defenseman with the Islanders since 1973, had been the team captain since 1978 and was one of the stars of his team and the league. Potvin skated a lap around the rink, holding the Cup high above his head. He then passed it to Mike Bossy, who had scored the series-winning goal. Bossy was an incredible scorer, some say the best ever. That season, he had 118 points and 60 goals in the regular season, and his teammates Bryan Trottier, John Tonelli and Clark Gilles had 34 goals, 31 goals, and 21 goals, respectively.

Bossy skated his victory lap, then handed the Cup to Trottier, his line mate. Trottier skated his victory lap with the crowd's deafening cheers continuing. As he ended his lap, he looked for the series MVP, one of the anchors of the team, Billy Smith, the brilliant goaltender and future Hall of Famer who played all four games of the series. As he handed the Cup to Smith, there was a crescendo of sound.

The Islanders began as an expansion team just eleven years earlier with the 1972–73 season, and now, with four consecutive Stanley Cups in eleven seasons, the players had success and fortune beyond their wildest dreams. With those four championships and a trip to the finals the following

Nassau County Coliseum in Long Island, home to the New York Islanders and the site of Dave Langevin and the Islanders' 1983 Stanley Cup triumph over the mighty Edmonton Oilers. *Wikimedia Commons.*

season—nineteen consecutive playoff series victories—no other professional sports team had reached that level, nor would one for the next thirty-eight years or more. This team was one for the ages.

Seventeen men played together on those Islander Stanley Cup championship teams. Five became NHL Hall of Famers: Mike Bossy, Denis Potvin, Billy Smith, Clark Gilles and Brian Trottier. Langevin had been an important part of the "smart first"[1] defense of Coach Al Arbour, contributing every other shift throughout the playoffs and in the final series sweep of the Oilers. For the series, Langevin had a +4 plus-minus rating, one of the best on the team. He was the team's tireless workhorse, playing in almost every game for those four regular seasons and in the playoffs. He played in 21 playoff games in 1980, 18 in 1981, 29 in 1982 and 8 in 1983. For the three preceding years, he played for the Oilers as a workhorse in almost every game and in 23 WHA playoff games. In his third season, 1979, he was selected as a WHA All-Star.

It had been quite a fantastic seven full seasons for Langevin, and the next season, his eighth, he would play another full season of 69 games and 12 playoff games. A further measure of Langevin's outstanding play and contribution in the playoffs was his plus/minus record for the five consecutive Stanley Cup playoffs. The plus-minus rating awards a plus to a player when they are on the ice when their team scores a goal and a minus when the player is on the ice when the other team scores. In these 78 games, Langevin was a +23. In his brilliant pro career, Langevin would play 729 total games and a monumental total of 110 playoff games: 87 NHL playoff games and 23 WHA playoff games. He had a string of six consecutive seasons of playing in the Finals, a total of 91 playoff games. Three of these six Finals were with Wayne Gretzkey on the ice, the first as his teammate in 1979 with the Oilers in the WHA Avco Cup Finals, losing to Bobby Hull and the Jets; the last two Finals with Gretzky as an opponent, sweeping the Great One and the Oilers, four games to none, in the fifth Finals and then losing to the Oilers, four games to one, in the sixth. In each of these three Gretzky-Langevin Finals playoffs, Gretzky led all scorers. In the 1978–79 season with the Oilers, Langevin played with Gretzky, who had joined the team as a seventeen-year-old (he turned eighteen halfway through the season on January 26). Gretzky led the WHA in scoring that season with 98 points. Langevin and Gretzky in the 1979 semifinals won a 7-game series against the iconic Gordie Howe and the Whalers. Howe was fifty years old, thirty-two years older than Gretzky, Howe was the holder of almost all NHL scoring records, including most times leading NHL playoffs in scoring (six), and was a twenty-three-time NHL All-Star. Gretzky was beginning his glorious career, on his way to becoming the greatest scorer of all time. Langevin had faced Gordie Howe in the regular season and in the playoffs in each of his three seasons with the Oilers, including his second season (1977–78), when Howe led the Whalers in scoring with 34 goals, 62 assists and 96 points. Langevin had a unique foundation-building experience for three seasons, playing against the most dominating scoring presence in Gordie Howe and for one season and two playoffs playing with and against Gretzky, the new dominating scorer who would rewrite the record book over the next fifteen years. On the night of May 17, 1983, Langevin was a seasoned player with equal or greater playoff experience than a number of the most experienced players in the league.

Langevin spearheaded the iconic Islander defense of Coach Arbour, stopping dead the record-setting Oiler offense. Arbour saw his team shut down the Oilers in Game 1 with Billy Smith's shutout. Game 2 saw Billy Smith slash Gretzky's legs and all the uproar it caused, yet the Oilers could not get one win in this best-of-seven series. In the four-year championship stretch, Arbour had the Islanders lead the league in 1980–81 with 110 points, and they finished first overall in 1981–82. The 1982–83 regular season was Arbour's tenth year coaching the Islanders.

MVP Billy Smith was finishing his victory lap with the Cup and looked for Langevin in the group of Islander players near the team bench and into their defensive zone. He wanted to give the Cup to Langevin. As a goalie, Smith knew Langevin's skills and excellence—he was one of the great defensemen in the league in clearing out players in front of the net. Smith wanted to show his gratitude for all that Langevin had done for him. There was no player more important than Langevin for allowing Smith to ply his trade as the best goalie in the NHL, to keep things clear in front of the crease and to direct traffic in front of the net, to break out of the zone.

On the ice for the Oilers that day were an incredible seven future Hall of Famers: Wayne Gretzky, Mark Messier, Jari Kurri, Paul Coffey, Glenn Anderson, Kevin Lowe and Grant Fuhr. The Stanley Cup Finals often feature the best of the best. The Montreal Canadian 1978 championship team had nine Hall of Famers; their opponents in the Finals, the Boston Bruins, had only two. The 2001–02 Detroit Red Wings also had nine; their opponent, the Hurricanes, had one. The 1983 Stanley Cup Finals must be near the top, with the Oilers' seven future Hall of Famers and the Islanders' five, a total of twelve. Most of them were at the beginning of their prime or at the zenith.

As Langevin carried the Cup through the neutral zone to begin his victory lap, he thought, perhaps, of his youth coaches on the east side of St. Paul; of skating as a ten-year-old on his outdoor neighborhood rink at Hazel Park, just east of White Bear Avenue; of skating for Coach Andre Beaulieu for Hill High School (renamed Hill-Murray School his senior year) on Larpenteur Avenue and North White Bear Avenue in the city of Maplewood, just across from Aldrich Arena, the home rink of his high school. Perhaps he thought of his four years at the University of Minnesota at Duluth with Coaches Terry Shercleffe and Gus Hendrickson. Now, looking across the rink to the Edmonton bench, he saw their head coach, Glen Sather, Langevin's coach the three years he played for the Oilers before joining the Islanders for the 1979–80 season. Especially clear was his senior year in high school as captain of his team, the Hill-Murray Pioneers, making the All-Conference Team with five of his teammates: Tim Whistler, Joe Nelson, Dick Spannbauer, Rick Belde and Scott Langevin, (Dave's brother, a sophomore). The team had only four losses all year against twenty wins, then four more wins in the playoffs. They won the Independent State Championship on their home rink of Aldrich Arena.

He had all of this in his head when he took his first full strides with the Stanley Cup. He began to raise it above his head. He was exhausted from head to toe. He could feel the lactic acid burn of physical exhaustion in his legs, shoulders and triceps, but he felt a small surge of energy that allowed him to skate around the rink—a lap for the Hill-Murray Pioneers, for the east side of the City of Saint Paul, for Hazel Park and for all of his teammates.

With four NHL championships, Dave Langevin reached a height very few NHL players reach. It is a feat that, at the time of this writing, no other homegrown Minnesota hockey great has achieved. A major part of those Islander teams, Langevin played almost every other defensive shift, killing penalties. He played in almost every game in each of the four regular eighty-game seasons and in almost every game in each of the playoff series. And this season, he was selected for the NHL All-Star team.

Holding the Stanley Cup, Dave thought back to eleven years earlier, his last high school hockey game, in the championships against Duluth Cathedral at Aldrich Arena on March 5, 1972, a 3–2 win. Then, he stood with a different championship trophy. On that day in 1972, Dave stood in the middle of a twenty-two-year "Golden Era" (1960–82) of Minnesota hockey—a time of building and broadening the foundation of hockey in the state.

Those twenty-two years was a transformative time, with a number of key figures especially the trio of John Mariucci, Lou Nanne and Herb Brooks. It was a time when several strong forces came together to substantially increase the quality of youth hockey and high school hockey that springboarded a number of Minnesota-grown players to the NHL.

By the end of the 1982–83 NHL season (referred to as "this season" in the following pages), Minnesota hockey had reached a zenith like no other time before. During that season or within a season before or after, thirty-one homegrown Minnesota hockey players, including Langevin, would play in many NHL/WHA games in their careers. It was a special time for Minnesota hockey: thirty-one strong, contributing players. It was a number that had never been reached before in the twenty-one-team NHL and would never be reached in the subsequent forty years, even with thirty-two teams. There was a very strong first wave of players in two seasons: twenty-one players in the 1976–77 season and nineteen players in the 1977–78 season. Both seasons saw strong players with careers of 200-plus, 300-plus and even 500-plus game careers. Twenty-five years after 1983, there was another strong wave of about fifteen to twenty Minnesota players, falling short of twenty-five and not coming close to the thirty-one of the glorious season of 1982–83. That first wave in 1977–78 comprised breakthrough players who put a hole in a wall that had stood for more than twenty years: the lack of American and Minnesota players, or very few. The thirty-one players of 1983 came through that hole and tore down the wall.

The peak of 1983 was further distinguished by three players being selected as All-Stars: Neal Broten, Mike Ramsey and Dave Langevin. The accomplishment was not achieved again until 2015. That 1983 season also saw a stretch of seven of the previous eight Stanley Cup champions featuring a Minnesota-grown player as a contributing factor. Bill Nyrop from Edina High played with the Canadiens in the first three of those years, and Langevin in the last four with the Islanders. In the next two years, Don Jackson of Bloomington Kennedy High won Cups with the Oilers.

Some of these men were in the prime of their careers that season; some were playing as the NHL's very best; and a few were at the end of their careers, not contributing a full season. Most played at least 500 NHL games, equivalent to about eight to nine seasons (60–80 games played per season). Several played more than 1,000 games, and most scored over 125 points. Minnesota NHL players during this time with fewer than 500 career games played are not included, with the exception of pioneer players such as Bill Nyrop. Langevin's 31 players of the 1982–83 seasons are:

MARK PAVELICH, A CENTER from Eveleth High (1976), was a talented, shifty skater; a gold-standard playmaker; and an Olympic gold medalist in 1980. He finished the 1982–83 season with the New York Rangers. Pavelich had his best NHL season that year, with 37 goals and 38 assists, finishing with 75 points in 78 games. The next season, he played 77 games with the Rangers and had his highest point total, 82 points and 29 goals.

Bill Baker, a defenseman from Grand Rapids High (1976), played the

Mark Pavelich taking the ice for the Rangers. Pavelich (Eveleth, 1976) is the Minnesotan with the most goals in his first two seasons with 70; 37 goals in one season; and two seasons of 30 or more goals. *Public domain.*

1982–83 season as a New York Ranger teammate of Pavelich, just as they had been teammates on the 1980 Olympic gold medal team. Baker had his best season that year, playing 70 games with 4 goals, 14 assists and 18 points as part of his four-season NHL career of 143 games.

Rob McClanahan, left-winger from Mounds View High (1976), was another New York Ranger and Olympic teammate with Baker and Pavelich. McClanahan had a strong year for the Rangers, playing 78 games with 22 goals, 26 assists and 48 points. It was his best NHL season. He finished his career that season with 224 regular-season games and 34 playoff games.

Aaron Broten, a center from Roseau High (1979), finished his second full season that year and the first of eight playing for the Devils.

Broten played 73 games and had 16 goals, 39 assists and 55 points, which led the Devils in scoring.

Mike Ramsey, a brilliant defenseman from Minneapolis Roosevelt High (1978), finished this season with 77 regular-season games and 10 playoff games at the other end of the state of New York, with the Buffalo Sabres. This was his third full NHL season after playing 13 regular-season games and 13 playoff games at the end of the 1979–80 season, immediately following winning the Olympic gold medal. In 1982–83, Ramsey, an established star of the league and an All-Star the season before and this season, had 8 goals, 30 assists and 38 points. He would finish his brilliant NHL career with four All-Star selections over eighteen seasons with a monumental 1,070 NHL games, 115 playoff games, 79 goals, 266 assists and 345 points.

Phil Housley, a gold-standard, goal-scoring defenseman and NHL Hall of Famer from South St. Paul High (1982), completed his first year in the NHL that season. It was an impact year as a teammate of Ramsey with the Sabres. Housley played in 77 games with 19 goals, 47 assists and 66 points. The next season, he had 31 goals, 46 assists and 77 points, all outstanding feats for a defenseman, especially in his first two years in the league, stepping directly from high school with no years of junior hockey or college hockey. Housley would play almost 1,500 regular-season NHL games over twenty seasons (ending in 2002–3) and 85 playoff games, scoring a total of 1,232 points. He held many offensive records. He was a seven-time All-Star and was inducted into the NHL Hall of Fame.

Reed Larson, a record-breaking offensive defenseman from Minneapolis Roosevelt High (1974), completed his sixth full season in 1982–83, playing 80 regular-season games with 22 goals, 52 assists and 74 points. The next season, he scored 23 goals amid a stretch of five straight over-20-goal seasons. He was an established star of the league, captain of the Red Wings, an All-Star in his first full season, the second American and first Minnesota NHL All-Star in the contemporary period, a four-time All-Star and the first American to score 200 goals. He is sixth all time among NHL defensemen in goals per game.

Neal Broten, center from Roseau High (1978), was in his second full season with the North Stars after playing with the University of Minnesota Gophers at the end of the 1980–81 regular season and for the playoffs up to the 1981 Stanley Cup Finals. In the 1982–83 season, he played 79 regular-season games with 32 goals, 45 assists and 77 points following a season of 38 goals, 66 assists and 98 points. Broten was an All-Star in this season, 1982–83. He played until 1996–97, accumulating sixteen seasons, 1,098

NHL regular-season games, 135 playoff games and 923 points. It was an incredible career that included a Stanley Cup with the Devils in 1995.

Dave Christian, a right-winger from Warroad High (1977), was with Broten on the 1980 Olympic team. Christian played this 1982–83 season, his fourth, with the Jets and served as their captain. In the previous year, he had 25 goals, and the year before, 28. The next season with the Capitals, Christian played all 80 games and scored 22 goals and had a total of 81 points.

Paul Holmgren, right-winger from St. Paul Harding High (1973), played 77 games for the Flyers that season with 19 goals, 24 assists and 43 points. Two years before, he scored 22 goals and was an All-Star; the year before that, he netted 30 goals for the Flyers. Holmgren would finish his great NHL career within a couple of years with a very strong 527 regular-season games and 82 playoff games and accumulating 144 goals, 179 assists and 323 points.

Tom Gorence, right-winger from St. Paul Academy (1975), played 53 games with the Flyers and was a teammate of Holmgren. He had 13 goals, 14 assists and 27 points. Two years before with the Flyers he played in 79 games and had 24 goals, 18 assists and 42 points. He finished his NHL career with 303 games.

Bill Nyrop, a defenseman from Edina High (1970), was, in 1982–83, one year removed from his out-of-retirement year when he played 42 games for the North Stars. A connection to Langevin's 1983 Stanley Cup championship is that it occurred five years after Nyrop's last Stanley Cup title with Montreal. It was his third Cup in three seasons with the Canadiens, playing in 72 regular-season games and 12 playoff games.

Don Jackson, a defenseman from Bloomington Kennedy High (1974), was on the same ice as Langevin that evening of the Stanley Cup Finals, playing for the Oilers. That season, Jackson played 71 regular-season games and 16 playoff games. The next year, Jackson—six feet, three inches tall and 201 pounds and possessor of a strong, defensive, physical style—anchored the defense for the Gretzky- and Messier-led Oilers's Stanley Cup title. The following season, Jackson won another Cup.

Russ Anderson, a defenseman from Minneapolis Washburn High (1974), was the captain of the NHL Hartford Whalers in 1982–83, playing 57 games. The next season, his last, he played 70 games with the Kings, finishing his career with 519 NHL games played.

Warren Miller, a right-winger from South St. Paul High (1972), graduated from high school the same year as Langevin. In this 1982–83 season, Miller played 56 games for the Hartford Whalers. He went on to play 500 professional games, 262 with the NHL and 238 for the WHA.

Jim Korn, a defenseman known for bone-crunching hits, was from Hopkins Lindbergh High (1975). He played all 80 games that season for the Maple Leafs after most of three seasons with the Red Wings. He would complete his NHL career with 9 seasons and 597 games.

Steve Christoff, right-winger from Richfield High (1976), played 45 games that season for the Calgary Flames with 9 goals, 8 assists and 17 points. The year before, he scored 26 goals and had 29 assists and 55 points.

Bryan "Butsy" Erickson, right-winger from Roseau High (1978), had his first year in the NHL the next season, playing 45 games with the Capitals with 12 goals, 17 assists and 19 points. He would finish his career with 351 games over seven seasons with 80 goals, 125 assists and 205 points.

Joe Micheletti, defenseman from Hibbing High (1973), the season before the 1982–83 season played 42 games for the Colorado Rockies and St. Louis Blues with 5 goals, 17 assists and 22 points, his last NHL season; two seasons before, he played 65 games for the Blues with 4 goals, 27 assists and 31 goals. Micheletti finished his NHL career with 300 games played, 158 in the NHL and 142 in the WHA.

Tom Kurvers, defenseman from Bloomington Jefferson High (1980), played four seasons at UMD. Two years after this season of 1982–83, he played 75 games for the Jacques Lemaire–coached Montreal Canadiens, scoring 10 goals with 35 assists for 45 points. The next season, Kurvers won a Stanley Cup with the Canadiens as the third-leading scorer among defensemen, behind Hall of Famers Larry Robinson and Chris Chelios. It was a great start to an excellent 12-year NHL career for this offensive defenseman with an incredible 659 regular NHL games played and 57 playoff games that included 93 goals, 328 assists and 421 points.

Scott Bjugstad, right-winger from Irondale High (1979), had his first year in the NHL in 1983–84 with the North Stars, playing just 5 games. The next season, he played 72 games with 11 goals, 4 assists and 15 points. In the 1985–86 campaign, he had a career-best 43 goals, 33 assists and 76 points. Bjugstad finished his NHL career with seven seasons and 317 games.

The next season, 1983–84, Jon Casey, a goalie from Grand Rapids High (1980), began his eight-season NHL career with the North Stars. He played four more seasons. His grand career included an All-Star selection in 1993.

A right-winger from Virginia High (1971), Jack Carlson played 54 games with 6 goals for the Blues that season. He had a hard-nosed, gritty style. The next season, his last, he played 58 games with the Blues for a career total of 508 games played over eleven seasons: 272 with the WHA (Minnesota Fighting Saints) and 236 with the NHL (North Stars and Blues).

Mike Antonovich, a center from Coleraine High (1971), in 1982–83 played 30 games for the Devils with Aaron Broten. One more year of 38 games with the Devils followed, ending a career of 573 professional games played (486 with the WHA and 87 with the NHL). He scored a total of 192 goals with 203 assists for 395 points.

Scot Kleinendorst, a center from Grand Rapids High (1978), played 30 games that season for the Rangers. He was just beginning an eight-season NHL career with 281 games played, including 26 playoff games. He had as teammates on the Rangers, Pavelich, Baker and McClanahan.

AN ADDITIONAL CONNECTION TO the 1982–83 season are five Minnesota NHL players who were winding down or ending their NHL careers without a full-season contribution. Some had exceptional skills and played well for a number of years before the 1982–83 campaign.

Defenseman Alan Hangsleben, from Warroad High (1971), ended his eight-year career with the Kings the season before, playing 18 games in a long career of 519 games in the NHL and WHA: six seasons with the Whalers, three with the Capitals and one with the Kings. He had 57 goals, 121 assists and 178 points. Hangsleben began his career in the pioneering times of the 1974–75 season.

Right-winger from Hastings High (1971), Dean Talafous ended his eight-year NHL career the season before, playing 29 games for the New York Rangers. His career of 497 NHL games included stints with the Flames, North Stars and Rangers. In 1976–77, he played 80 games for the North Stars and scored 22 goals with 27 assists for 49 points. For his career, he collected 104 goals, 154 assists and 258 points.

Tom Younghans, right-wing from St. Agnes High (1972), played 50 games the season before for the North Stars and Rangers, ending a career of 429 NHL games played over six seasons with career numbers of 44 goals, 41 assists and 85 points.

A left-wing from Robbinsdale Armstrong High (1973), Steve Jensen the season before played for the Kings, ending his seven-season career at 438 games played for the North Stars and Kings. He had three seasons of 20 or more goals.

Gary Sargent, center from Bemidji High (1972), in that same season played only 18 games. It was his last year in the NHL. His played 402 NHL games over eight seasons, three with the Kings and five with the North Stars.

THESE THIRTY-ONE PLAYERS FROM this amazing season included eighteen who played their high school hockey in the Minneapolis–Saint Paul area and thirteen who played outside of the Metro Area: seven from the Iron Range, three from Roseau, two from Warroad and one from Bemidji.

Another Minnesota connection to that 1982–83 season are two NHL coaches, Herb Brooks (New York Rangers) and Bob Johnson (Calgary Flames). Both were Minnesota-grown hockey players. They did not play their youth hockey before 1960. Brooks played for St. Paul Johnson High, graduating in 1955; Johnson played for Minneapolis Central High, graduating in 1949. They were nevertheless huge contributors to the twenty-two-year golden era. Brooks was one of the three foundational figures in the upgrading of Minnesota hockey in the golden era. Johnson did coach Minnesota high school hockey in this era, at Minneapolis Roosevelt High School for several seasons, taking the team to the state tournament in 1958, 1961 and 1963.

Johnson and Brooks were also monumental promoters and ambassadors of college hockey. They were the national faces and voices of college hockey through the 1970s and helped to grow the sport to a large degree in terms of game attendance and television, radio and newspaper coverage. Both men tirelessly gave high-quality seminars and clinics to Minnesota coaches of youth and high school hockey.

The 1982–83 season was Johnson's second coaching in the NHL. The Flames, whom he coached for five seasons, would go to the Stanley Cup Finals in 1985–86. In the 1982–83 season, the team lost in the Division Final to the Oilers. In his first season coaching the Penguins (1990–91), he led them to the Stanley Cup championship. Johnson's NHL coaching career followed a legendary sixteen-year college coaching career, beginning in 1963 at Colorado College and then at the University of Wisconsin from 1966 to 1982, winning three national championships there in 1973, 1977 and 1981.

Native Minnesotan Herb Brooks coached the New York Rangers for 285 games from 1981 to 1985, finishing with 131 wins, 113 losses and 41 ties. In that 1982–83 season, his second as an NHL coach, the Rangers finished with 80 points and lost in the first round of the playoffs. The season before, he was selected by the *Sporting News* as the NHL Coach of the Year. His NHL career followed his legendary feat coaching the U.S. Olympic gold medal

1982–83 NHL Season Minnesota Home-Grown Players and Coaches

All-Stars
Mike Ramsey – Buffalo Sabres (Minneapolis Roosevelt High, 1978)
Neal Broten – Minnesota North Stars (Roseau High, 1978)
Dave Langevin – New York Islanders (Hill-Murray High, 1972)

Head Coaches
Herb Brooks – New York Rangers (St. Paul Johnson High, 1955)
Bob Johnson – Calgary Flames (Minneapolis Central High, 1949)

Captains
Dave Christian – Winnipeg Jets (Warroad High, 1977)
Russ Anderson – Hartford Whalers (Minneapolis Washburn High, 1974)
Reed Larson – Red Wings, alternate captain (Minneapolis Roosevelt High, 1974)

Goal Totals
37 – Mark Pavelich – New York Rangers (Eveleth High, 1976)
32 – Neal Broten – Minnesota North Stars (Roseau High, 1978)
22 – Reed Larson – Detroit Red Wings (Minneapolis Roosevelt High, 1974)
22 – Rob McClanahan – New York Rangers (Mounds View High, 1976)
19 – Phil Housley – Buffalo Sabres (South St. Paul High, 1982)
19 – Paul Holmgren – Philadelphia Flyers (St. Paul Harding 1973)
18 – Dave Christian – Winnipeg Jets (Warroad High, 1977)
16 – Aaron Broten – New Jersey Devils (Roseau High, 1979)
13 – Tom Gorence – Philadelphia Flyers (St. Paul Academy, 1975)
12 – Butsy Erickson – New Jersey Devils (Roseau, 1978)
9 – Steve Christoff – Calgary Flames (Richfield High, 1976)
8 – Mike Ramsey – Buffalo Sabres (Minneapolis Roosevelt High, 1978)
7 – Mike Antonovich – New Jersey Devils (Coleraine, 1969)

Point Totals
77 – Neal Broten – Minnesota North Stars (Roseau, 1978)
75 – Mark Pavelich – New York Rangers (Eveleth High, 1976)
74 – Reed Larson – Detroit Red Wings (Minneapolis Roosevelt High, 1974)
66 – Phil Housley – Buffalo Sabres (South St. Paul High, 1982)
56 – Aaron Broten – New Jersey Devils (Roseau High, 1979)
48 – Rob McClanahan – New York Rangers (Mounds View High, 1976)
44 – Dave Christian – Winnipeg Jets (Warroad High, 1977)
43 – Paul Holmgren – Philadelphia Flyers (St. Paul Harding High, 1973)

team in 1980 and, before that, his time leading the University of Minnesota team (1972–79), with whom he won three national championships (1974, 1976 and 1979). Brooks's NHL career included three and a half seasons with the Rangers, one with the North Stars, one with the Devils and one with the Penguins for a total of six and a half seasons

Two Minnesota homegrown players as head coaches in the NHL in the same season—that had not happened before, and it has not happened since. There have been several homegrown Minnesota NHL head coaches, including Paul Holmgren, Todd Richards and Phil Housley, but never two in the same season. Bob Johnson was the first and only Minnesotan player to win a Stanley Cup championship as a coach (with the Pittsburgh Penguins in 1991).

The nature and magnitude of this special hockey season, this special time for prominent Minnesotans in the NHL, is further demonstrated by expanding the time span a few years and upping the criteria to that of All-Star selections. Before doing that, it should be noted that in the 1982–83 season alone, three of these players were selected as All-Stars, a record until thirty-seven years later, in 2015 (Dustin Byfuglien, Justin Faulk and Erik Johnson), then in 2016 (Byfuglien, Ryan McDonagh and Faulk) and in 2017 (McDonagh, Kyle Okposo and Faulk). From 1978 to 1986, seven different players were selected as All-Stars, for a total of twelve All-Star selections. No other period had as many different Minnesota players selected as All-Stars or as many selections in such a short time. It was another part of this groundbreaking group. The next best period, those grand seven years of 2009–18, saw six players and ten All-Star selections.

In the earlier group, Reed Larson was the first Minnesota homegrown player in the contemporary era to be selected an NHL All-Star and the second American NHL All-Star in the era. This was an incredible achievement, as he was selected in his first full season in the league after moving directly from college hockey. Two years later, in 1980, he was selected as an All-Star and again in 1981, joined by Paul Holmgren. They were the first Minnesota All-Stars in the modern era. Larson was an All-Star again in 1982. What makes his first selection even more remarkable is that his All-Star selection came in the midst of three dominating years of the Montreal Canadiens in the regular season and the playoffs. Montreal saw seven players selected for Larson's first All-Star team in the Wales Conference, greatly reducing the number of spots available for players from other teams. All seven of those Canadiens became Hall of Famers. Of the five defensemen on Larson's All-Star team, the other four were future Hall of Famers. Mike Ramsey, Neal Broten and Phil Housley were selected in their second full season in the league. In his first five full seasons, Larson was four times an All-Star. In Ramsey's first six full seasons, he was selected four times. And Housley had five straight seasons as an All-Star (1989–93). In his first eleven seasons, he was selected six times. These were phenomenal achievements so early in their brilliant and long careers.

A SECOND VISION, ANOTHER vision five years before Dave Langevin's moment on the ice, took place on Monday evening, Monday 22, 1978, at the Hartford Civic Arena. It was a few minutes after the end of the last game of the final series of the World Hockey Association's AVCO Cup. The Winnipeg Jets sealed a 5–3 victory over the Whalers and claimed the championship. On the bench of the losing team, the New England Whalers, most of the players were seated with heads down. They were tired and disappointed, having been swept in the series, four games to none. Seated at one end of the bench near one of the gates to the ice was Mike Antonovich, small in stature at five feet, eight inches tall and 175 pounds, but huge in heart and guts. He had incredible hockey skills, including stick-handling, shooting and scoring. His quickness and skill resulted in Antonovich creating space and scoring at a level that was not possible for most players. At the other end of the bench was hockey immortality, the league's leading career scorer and the holder of almost all offensive records: Gordie Howe. Also on the bench were his sons, defenseman Marty Howe and forward Mark Howe, both Americans who grew up in the Detroit area. Mark had a fantastic career to this date, including being a WHA All-Star. He continued for many years in a brilliant NHL career and was inducted into the Hockey Hall of Fame. Also on the bench was a center, Dave Keon, an NHL superstar for fourteen seasons (1960–75) with the Toronto Maple Leafs and a Calder Trophy winner as rookie of the year. He won two Stanley Cups and was a Hall of Famer. Keon finished second for the Whalers in playoff scoring, with 5 goals and 11 assists. In the regular season, he had 24 goals and 62 points.

Everyone on the bench was disappointed to be swept. They were feeling down, seeing their season this way. The team had the second-best record in the WHA that year, topped only by the Jets. Antonovich scored the first goal of the game shortly after the start, at 1:37 of the first period. It was the first time the Whalers had a lead in the series. But now Antonovich looked down the bench and saw Gordie Howe, and his disposition began to change. He felt better. This was his team, and here he was, having played for the WHA championship. It was an incredible, special season, with Gordie Howe at right wing, Mark Howe at left wing and Marty Howe on defense. Mike who joined the team before the start of the season, had a wonderful season, with 32 goals, second on the team to Gordie Howe's 34. Another accomplishment for Antonovich was his selection to play in the All-Star Game. The previous season, he had scored 40 goals with the Oilers, the Fighting Saints and the Whalers, Antonovich had an incredible 72 goals in these two years. Two seasons before, he had 25 goals, for a total of 97 goals in three seasons. As he was feeling better about himself, his team and this season, looking down the Whalers' bench toward Gordie Howe, he saw five other homegrown Minnesota players, all contributing to the team and the season. Antonovich played his high school hockey at Greenway of Coleraine in the pine forest, lake country of north-central Minnesota in the Iron Range. There on the bench were teammates from just down Highway 169 from Coleraine, 52 miles on the Iron Range to Virginia: forwards Jack Carlson (Virginia High, 1971) and his brother Steve Carlson (Virginia High, 1973), both six foot, three inches and 205 pounds. Steve had 9 points in the playoffs; Jack had 9 goals during the regular season. Farther down the bench was Tim Sheehy, from 117 miles north of Coleraine on the Canadian border. He was a high-flying right-winger at six feet tall and 185 pounds. A 1966 graduate of International Falls High, Sheehy assisted on the second Whaler goal to give the team a 2–0 lead. Sheehy had joined the Whalers that season for the last 25 games after playing 15 games for the Red Wings and 13 for the Birmingham Bulls. Sheehy had 8 goals for the Whalers in those 25 games and 4 points in the playoffs. The other Minnesota players were two stalwart defensemen. Alan Hangsleben (Warroad High, 1971), from the adjacent high school conference to the west of the Iron Range Conference, had 11 goals for the Whalers that season and 13 the season before. The very tough defenseman Bill Butters (White Bear Lake High, 1971), from the Metro Area, had played 45 games for the Whalers earlier in the season and did not finish with the team. The Whalers were an Iron Range Conference team, with four players from that conference.

Antonovich then turned to look out on the ice, and there was the title-winning team, the Winnipeg Jets, passing the AVCO Cup among themselves. Left-winger Bobby Hull handed the Cup to his center, Ulf Nillsson, who passed it to right-winger Anders Hedberg. This was the fourth phenomenal season for these three line mates with the Jets. (Hedberg and Nilsson were two of seven Swedes who had joined the team.) In their first season together, Hull led all Jet scorers with 142 points and a fantastic 77 goals. Nilsson was next with 120 points. Hedberg was third with 53 goals, 47 assists and 100 points. This season, 1977–78, Nilsson led the scoring for the Jets with 126 points. Hedberg was second with 122 points and 63 goals; Hull, third, had 117 points. In three of their four seasons together, all three players had 100 points or more. This championship was the second in three years for the Jets, having won in 1976 and making the finals in 1977, losing to the Quebec Nordiques. March Tardiff, left-winger with the Nordiques, won two Stanley Cups with the Montreal Canadiens in 1971 and 1973 and was the WHA's scoring leader that season with 65 goals, 89 assists and 154 points. He ended his WHA career first in career goals and second in points. Tardiff played 11 games in this season's playoffs. With all of the offensive skills, shots and scoring in the WHA playoffs, including from Hull, Hedberg, Nilsson, Gordie Howe, Mark Howe and Keon, as well as from Tardiff, Mike Antonovich led the playoffs in scoring. He had the most points and the most goals (10). This was an extraordinary achievement, and Antonovich let it sink in as he saw the three great Jet players celebrating. It brought a smile to his face. He, Mike Antonovich, among all these hockey greats, did it. He had led the playoffs in scoring.

He was celebrating the special, amazing, magical season: the All-Star Game, a great regular season and now leading scoring for the playoffs. Things had really come together in this, Antonovich's sixth season in the WHA. In his first season, he played 75 games for the Fighting Saints and had 20 goals. That followed three years of hockey for the University of Minnesota. His mind was reflecting back as he stood up and raised his stick as a salute to himself and to what he accomplished; a salute to his buddies growing up together back in Coleraine, Minnesota; a salute to his high school teammates; a salute to this team and his coach, Harry Neale, who was his coach in his first season with the Fighting Saints; a salute to all. He thought of playing pickup hockey, youth hockey and leading Greenway of Coleraine High School to three straight Minnesota State Tournaments in 1967, 1967 and 1968 under the direction of Coach Bob Gerander. In 1967, Greenway Coleraine won its first state championship, beating an undefeated St. Paul Johnson High team in the title game. The next year, the second championship, Antonovich was the leading scorer in the three-game tournament, with 3 goals, 6 assists and 9 points. For the Consolation Championship in 1969, Antonovich was the leading scorer of the tournament (7 goals, 1 assist and 8 points). In the 1969 tournament, Alan Hangsleben, his Whaler teammate in that special season and playoffs of 1978, played for Roseau, and Henry Boucha, Antonovich's teammate on the Fighting Saints, played for Warroad High. Another Whaler teammate from that season and playoffs, Bill Butters, played in the 1967 state tournament for White Bear Lake High School. In Coleraine, Minnesota, a town of almost two thousand people on Trout Lake, Antonovich had many achievements. But now, after this season and the playoffs, he was thinking of his teammates on those three state tournament teams. As he sat on the players' bench, he had a vision of the Minnesota homegrown players in that 1977–78 campaign, thinking of twenty strong, contributing players in the WHA and NHL. They all contributed to the groundbreaking, pioneering work of Minnesota players in the NHL. Some were WHA and NHL All-Stars. Most played 300 games or more; one played 904 games. They were part of the first strong wave.

Their effective play was pivotal in building a foundation for Minnesota players going forward, to the peak in 1983. They did this by proving their worth and being strong contributors to their teams. These twenty players did not have careers as long or as distinguished as the thirty-one players from the 1982–83 season, most of whom played more than 500 games (a few played 900 or more games) and many of whom were All-Stars. One player was a Hall of Famer. But those twenty played an important role in their careers of 200, 300, even 500 games. They were providing the building blocks before the era of the 1980 Olympic gold medal team, Houlsey and Kurvers. Many of these players started in the WHA in the early to mid-1970s and then transferred to the NHL. Among them were Paul Holmgren, who joined the Flyers late in 1976 from the WHA Fighting Saints. He played nine seasons for the Flyers and was an All-Star in 1981. Dave Langevin played three years for the WHA's Oilers and then went to the Islanders. Others started in the NHL, such as Henry Boucha with the Red Wings; Tom Younghans, Dean Talafous and Steve Jensen with the North Stars; Reed Larson with the Red Wings; and Bill Nyrop with the Canadiens. These twenty men were breakthrough players who broke the barrier to American and Minnesotan players in the NHL. The list that follows includes the nineteen players with their career stats played. The season listed refers to the player's 1977–78 season.

In the 1977–78 season, Antonovich thought of these twenty players, fifteen of whom were among those in the thoughts of Dave Langevin, who counted thirty-one homegrown players. So, about half of Langevin's players in the 1982–83 season comprised players from this first wave.

Four of the twenty were All-Stars, two in 1977–78 (Reed Larson and Mike Antonvich) and two in the next several years (Dave Langevin in 1979 and Paul Holmgren in 1981). One player won a Stanley Cup (Bill Nyrop).

- Reed Larson, defense, Red Wings. First full season for the Red Wings; 19 goals and 60 points; All-Star; 904 games.
- Mike Antonovich, center, Whalers. Sixth full season, for the Whalers; 34 goals in the regular season; All-Star; Stanley Cup Finals; most points and goals in playoffs; 573 games.
- Dave Langevin, defense, Oilers. Played in his second season; All-Star; WHA Finals; five consecutive Stanley Cup Finals; second All-Star selection in 1983 with the Islanders; 729 games.
- Paul Holmgren, right wing, Flyers. Played his second full season with Flyers; 16 goals; third season overall, first season with Fighting Saints; All-Star with Flyers; a 30-goal season in 1979–80; 578 games.
- Bill Nyrop, defense, Canadiens. Third season; Stanley Cup winner; three consecutive Stanley Cup Finals; 207 games.
- Bob Paradise, defense, Penguins. Seventh season; 368 games.
- Alan Hangsleben, defense, Whalers. Fourth season; season stats: 79 games, 11 goals, 18 assists, 29 points; 519 games.
- Bill Butters, defense, Whalers and North Stars. Fourth season, 45 games for the Whalers, 23 games for the North Stars 23; 289 games.
- Gary Sargent, defense, Kings. Third season; 7 goals, 34 assists, 41 points; 402 games.
- Warren Miller, forward, Oilers. Second season; 16 goals, 28 assists, 44 points for the Oilers and Nordiques; 500 games.
- Russ Anderson, defense, Penguins. Second season, 2 goals, 16 assists, 18 points; 519 games.
- Jack Carlson, forward, Whalers. Fourth season; 9 goals, 20 assists, 29 points; 508 games.
- Joe Micheletti, defense, Oilers. First full season for the Oilers; 14 goals, 34 assists, 48 points; 300 games.
- Steve Jensen, forward, North Stars. Third season; 13 goals, 17 assists, 30 points; 438 games.
- Tom Younghans, forward, North Stars. Second season; 10 goals, 8 assists, 18 points; 429 games.
- Dean Talafous, center, North Stars. Fourth season; 13 goals, 16 assists, 29 points; 497 games.
- Tim Sheehy, forward, Bulls, Red Wings, Whalers. Sixth season; 12 goals, 13 assists, 25 points; 460 games.

- Pete LoPresti, goalie, North Stars. Fourth season, all with the North Stars; 53 games, 12 wins, 35 losses, 6 ties; 175 games.
- Craig Norwich, defense, WHA Cincinatti Stingers. First season; 65 games, 7 goals, 23 assists, 30 points; 249 games.
- Steve Carlson, forward, Whalers. Fourth season; 6 goals, 7 assists, 13 points; 225 games.

The 1976–77 season was equally groundbreaking. In addition to the listed players, it featured Henry Boucha (283 games), Stan Gilbertson (428) and Mike Curran (130). The contribution was strong but not as strong as the 1977–78 season.

THE STORY OF MINNESOTA's homegrown hockey greats will be woven together with descriptions and insight from the unparalleled Lou Nanne. His hockey résumé is impressive. He was a college All-American and captain of the University of Minnesota Gophers. He was the captain of the 1968 U.S. Olympic team. He played eleven seasons in the NHL and served another ten years as an NHL general manger, including one as coach–general manager. Nanne received the Lester Patrick Award in 1989 for his efforts on behalf of hockey development in America, and he has continued in those efforts. Outside of the professional game, he has served as a TV analyst for every high school state tournament in Minnesota from 1964 to 2022.

Lastly, it should be said that this book focuses on homegrown Minnesota hockey greats in the National Hockey League. Except for occasional brief mentions, it does not cover high school, college or semipro greats. No doubt, these players were highly skilled and can be proud of their extraordinary accomplishments. They dominated high school hockey, scoring exciting goals for or against Hibbing, Eveleth, Elk River, Litchfield, Burnsville and Stillwater. They played brilliantly against elite teams to lead their own squads to conference championships or to state tournaments. For example, Dave Spehar scored a hat trick in three consecutive tournament games for Duluth East, and Kyle Rau scored a thrilling, gaming-winning overtime goal in the championship for Eden Prairie. Others dominated college hockey, playing for or against such storied programs as the University of Michigan, the University of Wisconsin, St. Cloud State University, Harvard and Boston College. Their stories are wonderful, and they are worthy of being told. But they are for another book at another time.

1

THE MEASURE OF GREATNESS

How does one measure greatness? What makes a hockey player great? What are the criteria to determine greatness?

To play in the NHL takes physical strength, durability, stamina, quickness, agility, mental toughness, focus and a mind for the game. It also requires skating skills—speed, turning, acceleration. It takes passing and shooting. According to Lou Nanne, the quickness and speed of the NHL game—the skating, passing, shooting—as well as the competition are so much greater than at the other levels. A player could be awesome in high school or dominating in college hockey, but it does not necessarily carry over to the NHL.

In the NHL a Minnesota player is competing with and against the best players in the world.

Wayne Gretzky, from Brantford, Ontario, and Jari Kurri, from Helsinki, Finland, both Hall of Famers, played alongside Don Jackson of Bloomington Kennedy High for the Oilers' Stanley Cup championships in 1984 and 1985. Playing against them were Jack Carlson of Virginia High, Mark Pavelich of Eveleth High, Dave Christian of Warroad High and Dave Langevin of Hill-Murray High.

Alex Ovechkin, from Moscow, Russia, played with T.J. Oshie of Warroad High and Matt Niskanen of Virginia High on the Capitals' Stanley Cup winners in 2018. Playing against them were Ryan McDonagh of Cretin-Derham High, Jordan Leopold of Armstrong High and Ben Clymer of Bloomington Jefferson High.

Patrick Kane, from Buffalo, New York, played with Nick Leddy of Eden Prairie High and Dustin Byfuglein of Roseau on the Chicago Blackhawks' championship teams (in 2010 for Leddy, in 2012 for Byfuglein). Opposing them were Casey Middlestadt of Eden Prairie High, Brock Nelson of Warroad High and Kyle Okposo of Shattuck–St. Mary's High.

Peter Forsberg, from Ornskoldsvik, Sweden, played with Shjon Podein of Rochester John Marshall High for several years with the Colorado Avalanche, including their Stanley Cup in 2001. Playing against him were Paul Martin of Elk River High and Phil Housley of South St. Paul High.

Guy Lafleur, from Thurso, Quebec, of the Canadiens was teammates with Bill Nyrop of Edina High. They won three Stanley Cups together in 1976, 1977 and 1978. Opposing them were Reed Larson of Minneapolis Roosevelt High and Henry Boucha of Warroad High.

With the Minnesota Wild, Marion Gaborik, from Trencin, Slovakia, teamed up with Darby Hendrickson of Richfield High. On the other side were Justin Faulk of South St. Paul High and Derek Stepan of St. Mary's Shattuck High.

Playing alongside Nathan McKinnon, from Halifax, Nova Scotia, on the Avalanche was Erik Johnson of Holy Angels Academy. Their opponents were Anders Lee of Edina High, Brady Skjei of Lakeville North High and Alex Goligoski from Grand Rapids High.

Red Wing Nicklas Lidstrom, from Vastaras, Sweden, was teammates with Craig Johnson of Hill-Murray High. They were opposed by David Backes of Spring Lake Park High, Mark Parrish of Bloomington Jefferson High and T.J. Brown of Rosemount High.

Mike Modano, from Livonia, Michigan, of the North Stars joined Neal Broten from Roseau High and goalie Jon Casey from Grand Rapids High. (Casey played with Modano for five years and against him for seven.) Playing against him were Tom Chorske of Minneapolis Southwest High, Trent Klatt of Osseo High and Chris McAlpine of Roseville High.

Mario Lemieux, from Montreal, Quebec, teamed with Jim Johnson from Robbinsdale Cooper High and Chris Dahlquist from Fridley High on the Penguins. Opposing them was Jamie Langenbrenner of Cloquet High.

Teemu Salanne, from Espoo, Finland, played with Ryan Carter from White Bear Lake High on the Anaheim Ducks' 2007 Stanley Cup team. On the other side of the ice were Tom Kurvers of Bloomington Jefferson High and Zach Parise of Shattuck–St. Mary's High.

On the Flyers, Bobby Clarke, from Flin Flon, Manitoba, took the ice with Paul Holmgren of St. Paul Harding High for nine seasons and Tom

Gorence of St. Paul Academy for five. Playing against him were Dean Talafous of Hastings High, Gary Sargent of Bemidji High, Tom Younghans of St. Agnes High and Steve Christoff of Richfield High.

Sergei Federov of the Red Wings teamed with Mike Ramsey of Minneapolis Roosevelt High, and playing against him, David Backes of Spring Lake Park High and Aaron Broten of Roseau High.

Pittsburgh Penguin great Sidney Crosby played alongside Matt Cullen of Moorhead High on the team's Stanley Cup victors of 2016 and 2017, and Jake Guentzel of Hill-Murray High won the Cup in 2017 with Pittsburgh. Playing against him were Nick Bjugstad of Blaine High and Patrick Eaves of Shattuck–St. Mary's High.

Auston Matthews played with fellow Maple Leaf Jake Gardiner of Minnetonka High. They competed against Blake Wheeler of Breck School, Brock Boeser of Burnsville High and Alex Stalock of South St. Paul High.

THIS BOOK FOCUSES ON NHL players, with a few exceptions. It includes only players who have established themselves as NHL veterans through the test of many seasons, roughly eight to nine, equaling about 500 games, 60 to 82 games per season.

Players who do not show up in statistics for goals and assists will show up for other reasons. Their teammates and coaches selected them as a captain or an alternate captain. They were an All-Star selection by fans, writers, teammates, coaches, opposing players or the league. The weight given to goals and assists leans in favor of offensive defensemen and offensive forwards. Defensemen who are highly skilled as *defensive* defensemen or forwards who are defensive or are superior checking forwards are recognized not with assists or goals but as All-Stars. For example, Dave Langevin, an iconic defensive defenseman, was recognized in 1983. Mike Ramsey, a defenseman, is a four-time All-Star and a team captain. He had many offensive skills with great stats but not high-scoring numbers. Ryan McDonagh, another steady defenseman with offensive skills, was recognized as an All-Star twice and was chosen by his coaches and teammates to serve as captain of the New York Rangers for four seasons. He now serves as an alternate captain of the Tampa Bay Lightning. Playoff goals and assists by forwards are other metrics.

2

A GOLDEN ERA THAT TRANSFORMED MINNESOTA HOCKEY

Minnesota youth and high school hockey before 1960 stood in stark contrast to the years between 1960 and 1982. Prior to 1960, there were few indoor arenas in the state. In the Twin Cities, there were six long-standing arenas: the St. Paul Auditorium, the University of Minnesota's Williams Arena, Minneapolis Arena, the Hippodrome at the Minnesota State Fair, the White Bear Lake Hippodrome and the Golden Valley Ice Arena, which opened only in 1958. Elsewhere, there were Roseau Memorial Arena (1949), Warroad Gardens (originally 1949, rebuilt in 1992), Hibbing Memorial Arena (1925, rebuilt in 1935), Virginia (1923), Eveleth Hippodrome (1922) and the Duluth Curling Club rink.[2]

In the twenty-plus years following 1960, indoor arenas in the Twin Cities multiplied more than tenfold, and Minnesota went from about 16 to 130, an eightfold increase. High school hockey grew from 75 teams to 154, more than a twofold increase.[3]

Overall, Minnesota State Hockey Tournament attendance went from about 45,000 to 80,000, then to over 120,000, from the St. Paul Auditorium to the Met Sports Center to the St. Paul Civic Center, respectively.[4] In 1967, the state got its first NHL team, the North Stars, which played at the Met Sports Center.

Developments beyond hockey were partly responsible for these tectonic shifts within the sport. The population of the Twin Cities grew 30 percent from 1960 to 1980, and Minnesota's population doubled from 1960 to 2000.[5] These increases, as well as that in the five-state area, stemmed from

Hibbing Memorial Building/Arena in Hibbing, Minnesota. It is one of the grand, original arenas in the heart of the Iron Range, built well before the golden era. *Myotus, Wikimedia Commons.*

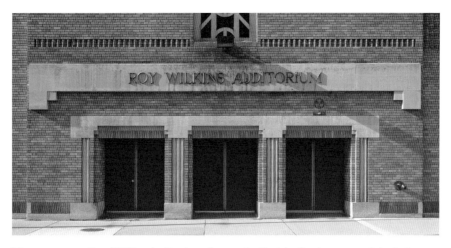

The entrance to Roy Wilkins Auditorium, former St. Paul Auditorium, one of the indoor arenas before the golden era, before 1960, and the home of the Minnesota State Hockey Tournament from its beginning in 1945 to 1968 before moving to the Met Sports Center. *Wikimedia Commons.*

Herb Brooks, 1983. Brooks (St. Paul Johnson, 1955) is a fountainhead figure in the golden era of Minnesota Hockey (1960–82). *Wikimedia Commons/Public domain.*

attractive employment options. There was great growth in employment with Medtronic, St. Jude Medical, Pillsbury, Target, General Mills, Carlson Companies, Toro and others. For example, from 1960 to 1980, Pillsbury saw a more than eightfold increase in employees, from 7,150 to 59,500, and General Mills had a more than fourfold increase, from 13,830 to 58,801[6]—a total increase of from 20,980 employees to 118,301.

On the ice, a gold medal in the 1980 Olympics and three college hockey championships in the 1970s from the Herb Brooks–coached Gophers added more energy and more impetus.

Also on the ice, but at a more individual level, John Mariucci, Lou Nanne and Herb Brooks were passionate and powerful ambassadors for the game in this era. Presidential historian Douglas Brinkley has written, "History teaches that zeitgeist sometimes develops around a fountainhead figure, that sometimes a transforming agent—in this case President Theodore Roosevelt—serves as an uplifting impetus for a new wave of collective thinking."[7] Similarly, around this trio, a zeitgeist developed, and the men became transforming agents for the development of Minnesota hockey players. Other important agents also emerged. They were outgoing personalities that connected with, motivated and challenged people—all for the development of Minnesota hockey. They pushed community leaders to make big decisions to start programs, fund programs and construct arenas. They inspired others to put up boards for outdoor rinks, to make phone calls to organize teams, to organize seminars and to train officials for the growing number of youth and high school games.

They did it all. Lou Nanne and Herb Brooks worked as counselors for a hockey camp (also called a clinic). Mariucci, the "Godfather of Minnesota Hockey," always a missionary for hockey, promoted Minnesota players to play college hockey and at the professional level. They were also big with the U.S. national hockey teams and Olympic teams. Brooks played for the 1964 and 1968 Olympic teams and for eight national teams, and Nanne played for the 1968 Olympic team.

The 3M/Mariucci Arena in Minneapolis. The arena is named for John Mariucci, the "Godfather of Minnesota Hockey" and a major figure of its transformation, along with Herb Brooks and Lou Nanne of the golden era of 1960–82. *Wikimedia Commons.*

John Mariucci graduated from Eveleth High in 1939. He played football and hockey at the University of Minnesota, leading the team to an undefeated AAU Championship in 1940. He played five seasons in the NHL for the Chicago Blackhawks (223 games) and served as captain in the 1945–46 season. Mariucci was a bruising, defense-minded defenseman known throughout the league. He played one season for the Minneapolis Millers, a minor-league team, and then retired after the 1951–52 season. Mariucci was the head coach of the 1956 U.S. Olympic team, winning a silver medal. When Herb Brooks become head coach, he brought an even more high-profile status to the program. With his personality and promotional skills, every game was highlighted. The series with the University of Wisconsin and Coach Bob Johnson, and the series with the University of North Dakota were set up as grand events, with huge promotions days ahead of the games. The games sold out and were watched in large numbers on TV and listened to on the radio. In 1966, early on in the golden age, the University of Minnesota–Duluth took big steps, with the construction and opening of the DECC, a beautiful, first-class arena near the Duluth harbor on the edge of downtown. There was a large increase in team in attendance, publicity and coverage on TV and radio. Summer hockey days camps were opening at new local rinks, as were summer overnight camps.

3

TWELVE BLUE LINERS

E leven NHL defensemen from Minnesota played youth and high
school hockey close in time and in place. The area is called the "Blue
Line Circle," or "Circle-11D." These players graduated from high
school between 1970 and 1982. A twelfth defenseman, Bob Paradise from
Cretin High School (1962), did some key early work in partly opening the
NHL gate for some of these defensemen and Minnesota players in general.
He was part of a small but significant first wave in the 1975–76 and 1976–77
seasons. Paradise came along eight years before these eleven defensemen and
from the center of the Circle-11D at Cretin High School. Paradise, at six
feet, one inch and 205 pounds, began his NHL career in 1971. By the end of
the 1975–76 season, he had played 268 games. He would play another 100
games to finish his career with 368 with the North Stars, Flames, Penguins
and Capitals. For almost all of these teams, Paradise was the only American;
all or almost all of his teammates were Canadians. For the twenty-eight
years beginning when John Mariucci played his last NHL game with the
Blackhawks in 1948 to before that 1975–76 season, there were only two or
three Minnesota players with substantial time in the league. One was Tommy
Williams, a forward from Duluth. His career spanned more than thirteen
seasons, with 664 games played and 430 points scored. Stan Gilbertson was
also from Duluth. Then there was Henry Boucha beginning in 1972. Now
within these two seasons, 1975–76 and 1976–77, ten strong players began
their play in the WHA and NHL such as: Warren Miller, Tom Youghans,
Dean Talafous, Paul Holmgren, Bill Nyrop, Steve Jensen, Mike Antonovich,
Russ Anderson, Dave Langevin and Reed Larson. The season before, Jack

Phil Housely is Minnesota's only player in the Hall of Fame in the contemporary period. He had a brilliant NHL career as one of the top offensive defensemen ever. Housley (South St. Paul, 1982) was a seven-time All-Star and played twenty-one seasons and 1,495 games. He scored 338 goals, 894 assists and a Minnesota-best 1,232 points. Housely had eleven seasons with 60 or more points. He was drafted sixth overall by Scotty Bowman and went directly from high school to the NHL, playing on the power play in his first game. *Paul Bereswill/Hockey Hall of Fame.*

Carlson, Bill Butters and Pete LoPresti began their careers, and one year before that, Tim Sheehy did. So, the number went from one or two players in the league for years at between fifteen and nineteen in two seasons. The numbers grew in the immediate two or three seasons that followed. Paradise was a college star in the Minnesota Intercollegiate Athletic Conference (MIAC) at St. Mary's College in Winona, Minnesota, from 1962 to 1966. He was undrafted and signed with the Montreal Canadiens after playing on the 1968 U.S. Olympic team with Lou Nanne and Herb Brooks, and he played on the 1969 U.S. national team.

The Circle-11D comprises a twenty-mile radius. The circle begins in the near northeast portion of the Minneapolis–St. Paul Metro Area at Aldrich Arena at 1850 North White Bear Avenue in Maplewood, just north of Larpenteur Street, St. Paul's northern boundary of East St. Paul. It extends almost directly south and a little west, ten miles across the Mississippi River to Wakota Arena (now Doug Woog Arena) on the river bluff of the city of South St. Paul, right above Concord Street and the historic stockyards along the river bottoms of the Mississippi. The border then moves directly west over the Minnesota River, past MSP Airport and a little south of I-494 a couple of miles to Ninety-Eighth Street, a total of twenty miles. It then extends to Bloomington Ice Garden off France Avenue South in southwest Bloomington, located just a mile from the bluffs of the Minnesota River. It then extends north and west seven miles to Braemar Arena, just off State Highway 169 on the very western boundary of the city of Edina on the western edge of Braemar Park. It then cuts a straight line from Braemar Arena east two miles to State Highway 100, north six miles to New Hope Arena and then east and north to Columbia Arena. The circle then continues back to Aldrich Arena.

In this circle, six classic community arenas served as critical venues, proving grounds even, for the development of these eleven players. All six arenas played a huge part in the twenty-two-year golden era. The three earlier arenas laid the foundation in the early 1960s. Aldrich Arena opened in 1962, then Wakota Arena (1962) and Braemar Arena (1965). Five years later, the Columbia Arena opened (1969), then the Bloomington Ice Garden (1970) and the New Hope Arena (1975).

In the span of twelve years, these eleven players would move to new venues. The arenas of their youth would be left behind for larger venues— homes of hockey royalty. Some would find their home ice at the Forum, in the heart of Montreal, Canada. Others moved to Olympia Arena, on the banks of the Detroit River in Detroit; Memorial Auditorium (the "Aud"), on the eastern shores of Lake Erie in Buffalo; or Nassau County Coliseum, on Long Island. Some moved to the Civic Arena (the "Igloo") in Pittsburgh, or Met Sports Arena in Bloomington, Minnesota.

These outstanding Minnesota players, all defensemen, played their youth and high school hockey in the circle from 1970 to 1982.

Bill Nyrop, Edina High School (1970) – 6'2", 205 lbs.
Dave Langevin, Hill-Murray High School (1972) – 6'2", 215 lbs.
Reed Larson, Minneapolis Roosevelt High School (1974) – 6'0", 195 lbs.
Don Jackson, Bloomington Kennedy High School (1974) – 6'3", 210 lbs.
Russ Anderson, Minneapolis Washburn High School (1974) – 6'3", 210 lbs.
Jim Korn, Hopkins Lindbergh High School (1975) – 6'4", 220 lbs.
Mike Ramsey, Minneapolis Roosevelt High School (1978) – 6'3", 195 lbs.
Tom Kurvers, Bloomington Jefferson High School (1980) – 6'0", 195 lbs.
Jim Johnson, Robbinsdale Cooper High School (1980) – 6'1", 185 lbs.
Chris Dahlquist, Fridley High School (1981) – 6'1", 196 lbs.
Phil Housley, South St. Paul High School (1982) – 5'10", 185 lbs.

These eleven players received excellent guidance from legendary high school coaches in the state and the nation. These coaches had college hockey experience, many serving as captains of their teams. One was an All-American for the Minnesota Gophers. Another won two NCAA National Championships with the University of Michigan. One was a member of a silver medal Olympic team. One coach also had national team experience. Another coached St. Thomas College for three seasons. And yet another served as an assistant coach for Bemidji State and the University of Minnesota. One coach led a junior hockey team to two national titles, and yet another won two Wisconsin State High School Championships as head coach. Within a few years after coaching these eleven players in high school, one became a head coach in the NHL, and one became an assistant coach of the U.S. Olympic team and then went on to coach the University of Minnesota for fourteen years. Others went on to brilliant high school success with numerous conference championships, state tournament appearances and state championships. These coaches saw many of their players compete at the college, minor-league and NHL levels.

These eleven players had numerous accomplishments and achievements in the NHL. Within a seven-year stretch, one of them won four Stanley Cup championships; another won three. One had 60 points his rookie season, the most by a rookie defenseman at that time. One was captain of the U.S. team in the inaugural Canada Cup in 1976. One had been an All-Star three times (1978, 1980 and 1981), another twice (1982 and 1983) and a third once (1983). Another played for the U.S. team in the 1981 Canada Cup. Another player, in his rookie NHL season in 1983, had 66 points. The next season, that same player had 31 goals and 77 points, followed by seasons of more than 60 points and, eventually, a season of 97 points. In the several years that followed the 1982–83 season, four of these players were All-Stars, several serving as captain of their team. In the next three seasons, one player had two Stanley Cups and another had one. By the end of these eleven players' NHL careers, one had played almost 1,500 regular-season games and 85 playoff games and tallied 1,232 points. This player was also selected as an All-Star seven times. Another player accumulated 1,070 games, 115 playoff games and 345 points. Yet another played 904 games with 685 points. The eleven players finished with a total of ten Stanley Cup championships and fifteen All-Star selections.

THE JOURNEYS OF THESE eleven players are connected to several of the most noted coaches, players and teams at the high school, college and NHL levels. The great coach Scotty Bowman played a prominent part for four of these players: Nyrop (three seasons and three Stanley Cup championships with the Montreal Canadiens), Ramsey (fourteen seasons with the Sabres), Housley (five seasons with the Sabres—only 12 games in the fifth season) and Kurvers (one season).

Several high-quality high school coaches prepared these eleven players: Willard Ikola of Edina High School, the most successful coach in Minnesota high school history; Tom Saterdalen of Bloomington Jefferson High School, a legend; and Doug Woog of South St. Paul. On many levels, one or more of the players had hockey experiences with Herb Brooks: Andre Beaulieu of Hill-Murray High School; Jerry Peterson of Bloomington Kennedy; Ken Staples of Cooper High School; Bucky Freeburg of Minneapolis Roosevelt High School and Dave Lund of Hopkins Lindbergh High School. Some played with and for Coach Al Arbour, Guy Lafleur, Larry Robinson, Serge Savard, Jacques Lemaire, Ken Dryden, Mike Bossy, Coach Glen Sather, Wayne Gretzky, Mark Messier, Lou Nanne (as a general manager and teammate), the 1976–77 Montreal Canadiens, the 1982–83 New York Islanders, the Minnesota Gophers and the 1980 Gold Medal Olympic team, among others.

Though these players came from different homes, their shared experiences demonstrate core factors that came together in their development: skating for hours at outdoor, neighborhood rinks; quality high school coaching; and the culture of the sport at the time, which gave them support and sparked joy.

The neighborhood outdoor rinks were their training grounds as well as their playgrounds. These included Arden Park in Edina for Bill Nyrop, Bromley Park in South St. Paul for Phil Housley, Running Park in Bloomington for Don Jackson, Hazel Park in St. Paul for Dave Langevin, Sibley Park in Minneapolis for Reed Larson, Hiawatha School Park in Minneapolis for Mike Ramsey and Kenny Park in Minneapolis for Russ Anderson.

One player, Bill Nyrop, had a home in a community of business executives and owners, doctors, dentists, accountants, professors, judges, lawyers and bankers. Edina was one of America's most concentrated high-income, professional cities. During Nyrop's youth and high school years, his father, Donald Nyrop, was CEO and chair of the board of Northwest Airlines from 1954 to 1976, transforming the company from a struggling, small airline to an international airline that was the fourth largest in the

United States. When Bill Nyrop arrived in Edina from Washington, D.C., in 1954 as a two-year-old with his mother, father and three sisters, the area was an established small city, Edina-Morningside, adjoining the southwest border of Minneapolis, a first-ring suburb of the city. During Nyrop's youth and teenage years, Edina would grow from a population of 9,744 in 1950 to 44,031 in 1970,[8] an almost fivefold increase in just twenty years. Edina had two very exclusive private country clubs, Interlachen Country Club and Edina Country Club, and a grand, twenty-seven-hole public golf course, Braemar. Another private club, Minikahda Country Club, was nearby just north and east of the city, a mile north up France Avenue in Minneapolis. Edina also had a robust retail area with a huge shopping mall, Southdale; a hospital, Fairview Southdale Hospital; medical clinics; major commercial retail developments; hotels; and banks. It also had offices for major corporations, mostly around Southdale and along I-494, I-494 and Highway 100. All of this development came after World War II, in Nyrop's youth. Edina of the late 1950s and 1960s added to the existing Edina-Morningside residential area.

The Nyrop family home was near the older neighborhood in the Edina-Morningside area just west of the Minneapolis border. Nyrop's game had a solid foundation of skills honed at the neighborhood outdoor rink near his home, about four blocks east, at Arden Park. He spent hours skating and playing pickup (not organized) hockey. One of his older sisters, Nancy Nyrop Scherer, remembers that the family would have to drag Bill from the Arden rink to come home for supper.

Nyrop moved into organized youth hockey via a strong Edina program. He played on a bantam travel team, the Edina Jaycees, that in 1967 won the State Bantam Tournament and then went to the National Bantam Tournament in Erie, Pennsylvania. They lost in the championship game to a Michigan team that had two players, Marty and Mark Howe (Gordie Howe's sons),

who went on to distinguished WHA and NHL careers. That 1966–67 bantam team was coached by Bud Sorem, a prime example of a tireless, volunteer, high-quality coach.

Coach Sorem represents coaches who were the foundation of great youth hockey programs in the late 1950s and 1960s in many communities throughout Minnesota, doing organizational work

Youth hockey official. *Patrik Yngvér/ Wikimedia Commons.*

such as registration, recruiting coaches, setting up clinics and purchasing jerseys, and, of course, coaching. Others were Bob Gunderson Sr. in Richfield and John V. Hoene in West St. Paul. According to the plaque on the John V. Hoene West St. Paul Arena, the latter "devoted his adult life to youth hockey." Coach Wes Barette on the east side of St. Paul and many more coaches were the bedrock of their communities' programs.

Well-maintained outdoor rinks were one of the symbols of this era in hockey-rich communities such as Hibbing, Duluth, Eveleth, Roseau, Warroad, South St. Paul, Edina, Bloomington, Richfield and Roseville and in Minneapolis neighborhood parks of the Southwest High, Washburn High and Roosevelt High areas. In addition, the east side of St. Paul had parks in the Johnson High and Harding High areas.

An incredible part of Nyrop's journey was that he and teammate Steve Curry were a defensive pair throughout some of their youth hockey and high school years and on their college team at Notre Dame. They led their high school team their junior year, 1969, to the Minnesota State Tournament Championship, the first for Edina, and in 1970, losing to Minneapolis Southwest High School, coached by legendary Dave Peterson, who would take his Southwest teams to fourteen state tournaments, be an assistant coach of the 1984 Olympic team and be a head coach of the 1988 and 1992 Olympic teams. In Nyrop's and Curry's second year at Notre Dame (1971–72), with Coach Lefty Smith, the team had a roster with eleven players from Minnesota, including two from Blake School (Ric Schafer and Mark Olive) and two from Hill-Murray High (Pat Conroy and Les Larson, who had been teammates of Langevin at Hill-Murray). The next year, their junior year, Nyrop was All-American. Two seasons later, Don Jackson arrived from Bloomington Kennedy High to play four years at Notre Dame.

THE JOURNEY OF THESE eleven remarkable defensemen moves fifteen miles east, from Nyrop in Edina to Phil Housley in South St. Paul. South St. Paul was an established, historic city and decidedly blue collar. It had stockyards, great schools, established banks, churches and a Croatian Hall. The city of South St. Paul was established in 1886 with 260 acres along the Mississippi River flats that comprised stockyards, slaughterhouses and meatpacking businesses that operated for over 122 years. The facilities were open seven days a week. But then it all began to decline in the late 1970s, '80s and '90s and shut down by 2008. At one point, the Armour plant alone had four thousand employees. Housley's home was in the community of America's largest stockyards in the 1960s and early '70s, larger than those in Omaha, larger than the stockyards of Chicago, larger than those anywhere else. The stockyards were the home of Hormel, Armour and Swift.

Many of Housley's neighbors worked in the stockyards, slaughterhouses and meatpacking plants or at the nearby St. Paul Park Refinery and Pine Bend Refinery (the largest in the five-state region). South St. Paul, on the south boundary of the city of St. Paul, was a city of 15,909 in 1950 and grew to 25,016 at the time of Housley's youth and then to 21,235 in 1980,[9] two years before Housley's graduation from high school. The city was the home of Harold LeVander, governor from 1967 to 1971, and Tim Pawlenty, governor from 2003 to 2011. Pawlenty, just a few years ahead of Housley in school, played JV hockey while Housley played varsity.

A key feature of the South St. Paul of Housley's youth is that it had a robust, excellent high school with many resources, great academics and many activities, including sports. The city recreational sports department had many strong programs, including hockey. This included well-run and well-maintained outdoor rinks and a landmark indoor rink, Wakota Arena, within miles of Houley's home and school. South St. Paul High School teams had a rich, deep history and tradition, enjoying many trips to the state tournament since it began in 1944. All of this was part of Housley's experience, part of his support, motivation and spirit.

Bromley Rink was Housley's primary outdoor venue, although he says he went to many outdoor rinks, including LaVander's pond. It was on these rinks that he honed his skills, spending hours learning the game. The Housley family home was about ten to twelve blocks from Bromley Rink, where Housley says he would "mostly spend nights there with my dad and brother, Larry. However, we would get dropped off there by Mom or Dad to play pickup with friends." He continues, "Bromley was a great rink because of the kids that hung out there. You did not want to shoot the puck over the fence on the north side of the rink because you had to jump over the boards and walk down a steep hill to retrieve your puck in the snow." He would skate with his buddies who lived on the north side of town with whom he played squirt, pee wee and bantam hockey, including Jonny Carlson, Herb Badalich, Paul Gallus, Dave Sobaskik Jaime Roberts and Al Niederkorn. Housley says he "liked all of his coaches growing up, each with their unique styles: Coach Tom Bohrer for Squirts; Coach George Powers for Pee Wees; Coach Paul Moen and Coach Dave Brodt for Bantams." These coaches are prime examples of the fantastic youth hockey coaches across Minnesota. In this case, they were coaching a future Hall of Famer. Housley's favorite outdoor rink growing up was at the high school, south of his home. The rink, according to Housley, had "great ice because they flooded late at night and I would have my mom drop me off at 7:00 a.m. and be the only one out there before the other kids would arrive. The ice was so nice to skate on very smooth." Housley was building his skating foundation. Brownley Park Rink is part of Kaposia Park at the southwest end of the park, bordering State Highway 52 on the west, Bromley Avenue on the south, then running four or five blocks east and then north to Butler Avenue and east down the ravine and bluff to Kaposia Park Landing on the Mississippi River.

THIS JOURNEY CONTINUES NORTH six or seven miles to Hazel Park on the east side of St. Paul. It zeroes in on White Bear Avenue and then east to Case Avenue and Hazel Park, the neighborhood rink of Dave Langevin. He spent hours skating for pickup and organized games. Hazel Park was Langevin's home, his rink. The area around Hazel Park features working-class neighborhoods with small commercial areas up and down White Bear Avenue. Across from the park's northeast corner is a 3M plant that extends for blocks. South a few blocks and a mile or two west was Hamm's Brewery. In nearby Phalen Park is the eighteen-hole Phalen Golf Course. Across the street from the west side of Phalen Park was Johnson High, where Herb Brooks played and lived nearby, as did Governor Wendy Anderson, who also played at the University of Minnesota and for the 1956 U.S. Olympic team. (He was the governor during Langevin's last two years of high school and in his college years.) Langevin's family home was near Hazel Park. From there, it was north up White Bear Avenue about two miles to Aldrich Arena for Langevin's high school practices and games. His high school, Hill School, was north up White Bear Avenue a little less than two miles to Larpenteur and then east a few blocks.

FOR TWO PLAYERS, REED Larson and Mike Ramsey, the journey continues from Hazel Park straight into the heart of a south Minneapolis neighborhood. They had their homes and their high school, Roosevelt High School, in residential, working- and middle-class neighborhoods. Roosevelt High was where former Minnesota governor Jesse Ventura graduated in 1969, five years before Larson. Growing up, the focus for Larson and Ramsey was the neighborhood park, where they learned to play hockey. Larson's neighborhood park was Sibley Park; Ramsey's was

Hiawatha School Park. Both were relatively close to their school, Roosevelt High School. Larson's rink park, Sibley Park, was located three blocks north of the northern boundary of Hiawatha Golf Course and eight short blocks, less than a mile, west of Roosevelt High School on Fortieth Street between Longfellow Avenue and Twentieth Avenue South.

Larson's family home was two short blocks from Sibley Park. The park's setup was similar to that of many outdoor rinks in Minneapolis—either as a separate neighborhood park or adjoining an elementary or junior high school. These facilities had a warming house, a flooded football field that was the "free skating" or "general skating" area, ice to the warming house entrance and a hockey rink or two. Throughout the day and evening, the rinks would have scheduled times for practices and games. Larson started playing on organized teams at Sibley Park at six years of age. He remembers that he "lived at the park" in the winters throughout his youth. He also recalls the park "having really good, hard, ice." On weekends, he would have a lunch packed, leave early in the morning and stay all day. This would include skating for hours on the football field, or free skating area. He also played pom pom, pull away, tag and crack the whip and hang out with girls and buddies. Many times, Larson would skate the football field with his hockey stick and a puck making long rushes with the puck or passing it, going the one hundred yards and back. There were pickup games on the rinks, and Larson, as an eleven- and twelve-year-old, was playing with high school players and older boys. The Hall brothers, who played for Roosevelt High, would skate at Sibley Park. When Larson was in his preteen years, his buddies had an arrangement with the rink attendant. At closing time at 9:00 p.m., the attendant would kick everyone out of the warming house, clean and lock up and turn off all the lights, including the huge floodlights that lit the whole park. Then he would turn on all the lights throughout the park and allow Larson and his buddies to skate, as long as they turned off the lights and locked the warming house when they left. They would have the whole rink to themselves from 9:00 p.m. to 11:00 or 11:30 p.m. or even midnight—an additional one or two hours or more of ice time. Sibley Park was a paradise for Larson. He built his hockey foundation of skating, puck-handling and shooting skills. His first bantam coach was Dave Benolkin, who moved Larson's progress forward. Larson's first year on the varsity team at Roosevelt High was in tenth grade. That season, the team's practices were split between outdoor and indoor sessions. Over the next two years, indoor practices became more common. The team's outdoor practices were mostly at Sibley Park and at Lake Hiawatha Park Rink. Indoor sessions were at Minneapolis Auditorium, Breck Arena and, on occasion, at Met Sports Center, where the North Stars played.

Mike Ramsey's rink park, Hiawatha School Park Rink, was located east of Roosevelt High School. It was across Hiawatha Avenue and Minnehaha Avenue, on Forty-Second Street on its north side, Forty-Second Avenue South on the west and Forty-Fourth Avenue South on the east side. It was about a mile and a half, or fourteen blocks, east on Forty-Second Street from Roosevelt High School.

In their pee wee and bantam years, Larson and Ramsey had practices and games at the Breck Rink/Arena, which was close for Ramsey, only a few blocks from Hiawatha School Park, and farther away for Larson from Sibley Park. From the late 1960s through the mid-1970s, the Breck Rink/Arena had an indoor arena with a large, wooden, curved roof. It was open on the east end, with natural ice that was managed by Jack Blatherwick, the Breck head coach from 1964 to 1975. Blatherwick would go on to get his doctorate in kinesiology from the University of Minnesota and be a contributing consultant to Herb Brooks with the university in the late 1970s and with the 1980 U.S. Olympic team. He also served for decades as a conditioning coach and consultant for NHL teams.

THE JOURNEY CONTINUES FROM Sibley Park and Hiawatha School Park to Kenny Park in Minneapolis, the neighborhood rink of Russ Anderson. This is where Anderson played pickup and organized hockey for Coach Olive. Kenny Park is in a residential area of modest homes five to seven blocks south of the larger, upper-tier homes along the Minnehaha Creek area and a few blocks north to the area surrounding Lake Harriet. Kenny Park is located about three miles east and a little south from Arden Park, the neighborhood rink of Bill Nyrop. Kenny Park is only three to four blocks from the southern boundary of the cities of Minneapolis and Richfield.

THROUGH THE CITY OF Richfield, the journey moves south to Bloomington, where Don Jackson and Tom Kurvers attended Bloomington Kennedy High School and Bloomington Jefferson High School, respectively. There was a third high school in the central part of the city, Bloomington Lincoln High School (1965–82). It had great hockey teams under Coach Terry Bergstrom, going to the Minnesota State Tournament in 1975. Bloomington is a post–

World War II suburb of Minneapolis. It continued Minneapolis's street grid to the south after the streets run through Richfield, especially in the east and central parts of Bloomington. In western Bloomington, the Bush Lake area has upper-tier houses along the park and rolling, wooded hills; the central and eastern areas north of the Minnesota River bluffs are home to middle-class families in rows of single-family homes. Large office, retail and hotel developments took place on the north end of the city along I-494, such as Southtown Shopping Mall. On the eastern edge of the city was Met Sports Center. The home, beginning in 1967, of the Minnesota North Stars was only a couple of miles from the home and high school of Don Jackson. Next to Met Sports Center, constructed more than eight years before, was Met Stadium, the home of the Minnesota Twins and the Minnesota Vikings. The city had several neighborhood commercial areas along Old Shakopee Road on the south side and at intersections such as Lyndale Avenue South and Ninety-Eighth Street near Bloomington Kennedy High, and at France Avenue and Old Shakopee Road just south of Bloomington Jefferson High. A textbook example of the postwar baby boom, Bloomington's population grew from 9,902 in 1950 to 81,897 in 1970,[10] a more than eightfold increase.

The Jackson family home was close to Bloomington Kennedy High. Running Park, the neighborhood outdoor rink, was where Jackson put in hours of skating and pickup hockey. Before his sophomore year, he had a growth spurt. During tryouts his sophomore year and throughout the season, he was a tall, lanky and slightly uncoordinated defenseman, says his coach, Jerry Peterson. Yet at the start of the season Peterson threw Jackson in as one of four defensemen who played regular shifts all year. With this experience, Jackson grew step by step and began his significant improvement. By his senior year, he was the "top defenseman in the state," according to Peterson. There may not have been a greater improvement in two years than Jackson's. He became excellent at leading a rush. In college at Notre Dame, he became tough and added a very defensive part to his game, playing the position increasingly well.

THESE PLAYERS RECEIVED THE highest-quality high school guidance from some of the most renowned and accomplished coaches in Minnesota and in the country. They brought to their teaching of these eleven players a background of deep, varied playing and coaching experience.

Willard Ikola coached Bill Nyrop at Edina High School from 1967 to 1970. Ikola brought a depth of state high school tournament, college and

Boys' 2020 high school championship game between Hill-Murray and Eden Prairie at Xcel Energy Center in St. Paul. Hill-Murray High is the alma mater of All-Star and Stanley Cup champion Dave Langevin and Craig Johnson; Eden Prairie High, that of Stanley Cup champion Nick Leddy. *Wikimedia Commons*.

Olympic experience to his first and only high school coaching position, which lasted from 1958 to 1991. Nyrop's first year playing for Edina was as a tenth-grader for the 1967–68 season. In his junior year, he led his team to its first Minnesota State High School Championship. Nyrop and Coach Ikola started an iconic, hockey-rich tradition and one of the historic runs of high school hockey championships with Edina, albeit rivaled by several other schools, including Langevin's Hill-Murray. Ikola would end his coaching career with eight state championships, eighteen section titles, twenty-two conference championships (Lake Conference) and a 616-149-38 record that is the third best in the nation and good for the second most wins in Minnesota. Ikola was named the Minnesota High School Coach of the Year six times.[11] Some of Nyrop's teammates and numerous players in years to come would play Division I college hockey; some would play in the NHL.

Coach Ikola brought the hockey tradition and mindset of the Iron Range of Minnesota, specifically Eveleth, the mining town of his youth, to Nyrop and his teammates in Edina. They absorbed all of it and developed a hard-hitting, fast-skating brand of hockey built on discipline and hard work. Nyrop each week figuratively lived on the Iron Range for two to three hours of practice a day, six days a week for three to four months of the hockey season. Coach Ikola had been a goalie for Eveleth High School, leading his team to three undefeated seasons and three Minnesota State High School Hockey Tournament (MSHST) championships (1948, 1949 and 1950). He then played goalie for two years for the University of Michigan, winning national championships both years (1951 and 1952). He was also the goalie for the United States in the 1956 Olympics in Cortina, Italy, leading the team to a silver medal by beating Canada in the semifinals. On his coaching in Edina and building the foundation for the twenty-two-year golden era and Nyrop in particular, Ikola said in 2020: "Once we got indoors [with the opening of Braemar Arena in 1965] our kids came out of youth programs with better skills. And that's when the high school program took off."

Andre Beaulieu coached Dave Langevin at Hill-Murray High (Hill High until the 1971–72 season) for his three seasons (1968–72). Coach Beaulieu came from Montreal and junior hockey there as a center and played at St. Mary's College in Winona, Minnesota, for four years (1961–64), winning the league scoring title all four years. He was a four-time All-Conference selection and was the highest-scoring player in all collegiate hockey during those years. Beaulieu brought to his first high school coaching job the experience of junior hockey in Montreal and a brilliant small-college career at St. Mary's. Within a year of Langevin graduating, Beulieu was coaching junior hockey, the Minnesota Junior Stars, and within five years, he was an NHL assistant coach, then a head coach for 32 games in the 1997–78 season, all with the North Stars. Beaulieu coached at Hill-Murray for four years, establishing an incredible record of two state independent championships in 1970 and 1972 and conference championships each year. His teams were dominant, with a hard-checking, stifling defensive style. The 1970–71 team allowed only 32 goals in 28 games and ended with a 26-1-1 record. A number of the team's players went on to Division I hockey. Herb Brooks called that team "probably the best four defensemen a high school team ever had."[12] Les Larson was paired with Langevin that year.

Langevin's high school teams scrimmaged with many of the best teams. Langevin stated: "Andre was a big proponent of using the scrimmage. We would have two or three scrimmages a week. We would go all over the city and play the top teams."[13] In a high school hockey season, if scrimmages were considered somewhat equivalent to a game, this would add 10 to 12 games over ten to twelve weeks to a 20- to 26-game season, for a total of 30 to 38 games.

Another proponent of scrimmages was the brilliant Joe Zywiec, head coach of Henry Sibley High School for ten years beginning with the 1977–78 season. (Coach Doug Woog's first season was as head coach of rival South St. Paul.) Zywiec took his team to the Minnesota State Tournament in 1982 and 1983, taking third place in 1983. He was one of the smartest, most instructive and most focused and prepared coaches. His high-energy practices were heavy on drills, one right after the other. Coach Zywiec scheduled scrimmages on Mondays from late afternoons to early evenings after the team's regular Monday practices. He would schedule scrimmages with teams that Sibley was not scheduled to play, including some of the best teams in the Metro Area. Sibley played games on Thursday and Saturday evenings. It was a fantastic coaching and teaching schedule, having a practice each day for three days plus a scrimmage with two practices that followed and preceded the first game of the week and then a practice after the first game and before the second game of the week.

Zywiec kept practice drills on index cards, each drill on a different card. He had over five hundred cards. Zywiec played college hockey as a center at Bemidji State University for Coach Bob Peters from 1969 to 1972. Peters had recently come to Bemidji State from Division I University of North Dakota, where he had been head coach for two seasons (1964–66), winning the McNaughton Cup one year. A grand coaching tree sprang from players who had played for Peters. Terry Bergstrom of Bloomington Lincoln took his team to the 1975 Minnesota State Tournament. Gary Hokanson coached at Roseau for twelve years (1977–90). Joe Zywiec was at Sibley. And Dennis Schueller coached at Simley High School in Inver Grove Heights. Coach Peters had a number of rules, tricks and styles for his players, and these were adopted by his former players when they became coaches. The ideas included both big things and small things, like using only black tape on the blades of the players' sticks so that it would be more difficult for a goalie to pick up the puck.

Langevin also benefited from Assistant Coach Dick Paradise in Langevin's tenth-grade year, the 1969–70 season. Paradise, from Cretin High School (1963), had a great career as a big defenseman for the Minnesota Gophers through 1965–68. The year after his time coaching Langevin, he began playing in the WHA with the Minnesota Fighting Saints at the St. Paul Civic Center, just five miles from Langevin's high school. Dick Paradise's brother Bob, also from Cretin High School (1962), played four years at St. Mary's College and played with Lou Nanne and Herb Brooks on the U.S. Olympic team in 1968 in Grenoble, France. He played 368 NHL games with the North Stars, Penguins and Capitals.

Langevin credits Beaulieu more than any other coach for his development. "He brought me to a different level through hard work, teamwork, and accountability as a player which is the foundation of playing well."[14] Beaulieu and Langevin for their four and three years, respectively, at Hill-Murray High

School were in the midst of a decade-long dynasty in Catholic Conference Championships and Minnesota State Independent Championships that laid the foundation for one of the state's best high school hockey programs over the next forty years.

Clayton "Bucky" Freeburg, the coach at Minneapolis Roosevelt High School, had Reed Larson for three seasons (1971–74) and Mike Ramsey for three seasons (1975–78). Freeburg brought a depth of coaching philosophy and experience from his college days as captain of the St. Cloud State University team in 1959 and from twenty years as head tennis coach at Roosevelt. He also served as an assistant hockey coach at Roosevelt and gained Minnesota State Hockey Tournament experience from the Roosevelt team he coached in 1966–67.[15] He then had five seasons of experience up to the time of Reed Larson's first year, and another four seasons up to Mike Ramsey's first year. The highly competitive Minneapolis City Conference included Dave Peterson's Southwest High teams, a tough Washburn High team, a West High team coached by legendary Jim Baxter and, on occasion, South High.

Mike Ramsey commented on the coaching style of Freeburg: "Bucky was very innovative, a little ahead of his time there. After years of playing in the NHL I realized the stuff we were doing [at Roosevelt with Coach Freeburg] was ahead of our time."[16] Freeburg's Roosevelt teams were in the MSHST in 1967, 1974 and 1978 and were conference champions in 1973, 1974 and 1978. Coach Freeburg was inducted into the Minnesota Hockey Coaches Association Hall of Fame in 2015. He is the only Minnesota high school hockey coach in the contemporary period to coach two players who later were multiple NHL All-Star selections (Larson and Ramsey). Tom Ward of Shattuck–St. Mary's is the only other man to coach two later NHL All-Stars (Zach Parise and Kyle Okposo).

Doug Woog was Phil Housley's coach at South St. Paul High School. Housley's first year on the team was Woog's second as the school's coach. Woog brought experience playing for the U.S. national team in 1966–67 and playing center for the University of Minnesota. He had also coached at the junior hockey level, as assistant coach to Herb Brooks with the Minnesota Junior Stars and as head coach of the St. Paul Vulcans junior hockey team.[17] In addition, Woog brought incredible accomplishments as a high school player, having led South St. Paul High School to four state tournaments. He was on the All-Tournament Team in three of the four tournaments and in 1962 was the leading scorer in the tournament. Woog worked his team hard to get better. Following a game or a practice, if the effort was not there from the players, Woog often directed the team bus to stop at the outdoor rink next to the school, and the team would skate and do drills to right the ship.

Housley excelled, benefiting from the great hockey mind of Coach Woog. Housley was also fortunate to have Assistant Coach Donald "Whitey" Willer. Willer had been head coach for several years of Brady High School, leading it to third place in the 1972 State Independent Tournament. Dave Langevin was playing for Hill-Murray, which won the tournament, and Tom Gorence was playing for St. Paul Academy. Willer was also head coach at St. Thomas Academy, taking them to the Minnesota State Independent Tournament in 1971 and 1970, winning consolation in 1970. Coach Willer, similar to Woog, grew up in South St. Paul and played hockey for South St. Paul High. Willer played in the state tournament in 1953. During Housley's senior year, Woog was an assistant coach for the 1982 U.S. World Junior team, which Housley was a member of. Two years after Housley graduated, Woog was an assistant coach of the 1984 U.S. Olympic hockey team. During his six years coaching South St. Paul High School, his teams won two conference titles and went to the state tournament four times.

According to Phil Housley, "Coach Woog was ahead of his time and would give me pointers about the game....He did challenge me and pushed me a bit harder than the other players on the team, because he kept wanting me to get better."

Coach Woog knew everyone in South St. Paul. He was very personable as a youth growing up in the city, and his father was the longtime manager of a social club, Croatian Hall. Woog played four years of high school hockey as well as other sports and served as a counselor at South St. Paul High. His sons played high school for him at South St. Paul. Hockey coaches are next to God, and their service to their players, to their school, to fellow teachers and students and to their community is a huge force for good. Woog exemplified this. Many hockey coaches know their community well, but it is hard to think of anyone who knew the people of his community better than Woog did.

Phil Housley went directly from playing for one of the great high school coaches to playing for the greatest NHL coach, Scotty Bowman. Within three years of Housley graduating and one year after serving as the assistant U.S. Olympic hockey coach, Woog became head coach of the University of Minnesota men's team, which he led successfully for fourteen years. He was inducted into the Minnesota Hockey Coaches Association Hall of Fame in 2003 and into the U.S. Hockey Hall of Fame in 2002. Willer was inducted into the Minnesota Hockey Coaches Association Hall of Fame in 1995. Of the eleven players we are highlighting, Woog is the only one of their high school coaches to do so in the community they grew up in and at the same high school they played for.

Tom Saterdalen was the coach of Tom Kurvers at Bloomington Jefferson High School. Saterdalen brought an exceptional pedigree to the school. He had been head coach of Superior, Wisconsin High School, winning two Wisconsin State High School Championships. Before that, he was an assistant coach at Bemidji State (1965–66) and an assistant coach for the University of Minnesota Gophers (1970–73). Saterdalen played hockey at Rochester John Marshall High School and at Bemidji State, where he was captain of the team his senior year.

There are many wonderful high school head coach–assistant coach duos. Coach Saterdalen had Assistant John Bianchi and, for a short tenure, Assistant Coach Mike Thomas (who served as head coach for Richfield High School and coached at Eagan High School). Bianchi was a longtime teacher and later served as an interim principal at Jefferson High School and at several other schools in the Minneapolis–St. Paul Metro Area, including Minnetonka High School and St. Paul Humboldt High School. During his twenty-nine-year head coaching career at Jefferson High School (1973–2002), Saterdalen had sixty-five players go on to Division I hockey, a phenomenal record. His career coaching record is 703-228-28 at Jefferson and 545-167-21 at Minnesota and included thirteen Lake Conference titles, fifteen section titles, five state titles and three state third-place finishes. He was named Minnesota Hockey Coaches Association Coach of the Year four times, Section Hockey Coach of the Year six times and Gunderson Lake Conference Coach of the Year four times.[18] Saterdalen was inducted into the Minnesota Hockey Coaches Association Hall of Fame in 2005. Assistant Coach John Bianchi was inducted into the Minnesota Hockey Coaches Association Hall of Fame in 1999.

Jerry Peterson was the coach of Don Jackson at Bloomington Kennedy High School for Jackson's three years from 1971 to 1974. Peterson had a legendary career at Bloomington Kennedy over twenty-five seasons. From 1967 to 1992, he took his team to the state tournament six times, winning it in 1987 (second place in 1984 and consolation in 1976). He amassed a record of 369 wins, 222 losses and 22 ties. Peterson played center as a four-time All-Conference MIAC player and was captain of the Augsburg College team. He played high school hockey at Minnehaha Academy for Coach Jim Baxter for three years, leading his team to the Prep School Hockey Tournament three years in a row. Peterson was inducted into the Minnesota Hockey Coaches Association Hall of Fame in 1995.

Ken Staples coached Jim Johnson at Robbinsdale Cooper High School from 1977 to 1980. In high school, Staples played terrific hockey, including being an All-Conference/All-City player for three years at St. Paul Humboldt High School. After high school, he was offered a contract by the NHL's Blackhawks but chose to play baseball, signing with the Brooklyn Dodgers. He coached three seasons of Division III hockey at St. Thomas College beginning in 1956 and amassed an overall record of 60 wins and 20 losses and a MIAC championship. For fifteen years beginning in 1959, he was the head JV hockey coach at Robbinsdale Cooper High School and began eleven seasons as head varsity coach at Robbinsdale Cooper (1975–86), ending with a record of 151-78-5. His record in the Lake Conference was 120-66-5, twice winning a Lake Conference championship.[19]

Staples was a taskmaster who conducted challenging practices. In this coaching, including his seasons as a college hockey coach, he brought tremendous results to his player, Jim Johnson. Staples was inducted into the Minnesota Hockey Coaches Association Hall of Fame in 2006.

ONE OF THE DIFFERENCES among the eleven players was their routes from high school hockey to the NHL. Some took the then more traditional, now unusual, step of playing four years of college hockey. Some went directly from the Olympic ice to the NHL. Others skated from the middle of a college hockey season to the NHL. One player went from high school to the NHL without playing any junior hockey or select team training seasons.

Nyrop, Langevin, Jackson, Korn, Johnson, Dahlquist and Kurvers each played four seasons of college hockey. Nyrop and Jackson played at Notre Dame. Langevin, Johnson and Kurvers attended the University of Minnesota–Duluth. Korn played four seasons at Providence College in Rhode Island. Dahlquist played four years at Lake Superior State. Nyrop and Jackson played for Coach Lefty Smith at Notre Dame. Smith had been the coach at South St. Paul High School, Phil Housley's school, and left in 1968 to start the hockey program at Notre Dame. After completing his four years at Notre Dame, Nyrop played a season for the Montreal Canadiens' minor-league team, the American Hockey League's Nova Scotia Voyageurs. The next season, he was called up on February 24, 1976, becoming a regular member for the remaining nineteen games of the regular season and thirteen playoff games on the way to a Stanley Cup. Langevin played for Terry Shercliffe and Gus Hendrickson at UMD. He was All-WCHA and All-American second team and scored nineteen goals his senior season, a record for defensemen that at the time of this writing still stands.

Kurvers played for Hendrickson and Mike Sertich at UMD and, in 1984, his senior year, won the Hobey Baker Award as the most outstanding player in college hockey, scoring 75 points. Kurvers was All-WCHA and All-American. Johnson played four seasons at UMD for Hendrickson and Coach Sertich following one year of junior hockey. Jim Korn went directly from Hopkins Lindbergh High School in 1975 to playing for Coach Lou Lamoriello at Providence College and then to the Detroit Red Wings. Korn would play three seasons for Lamoriello and the New Jersey Devils.

Reed Larson went from Minneapolis Roosevelt High School in 1974 to playing for Coach Herb Brooks at the University of Minnesota, winning a national championship in 1976. More than halfway through his third season, he went to the NHL, playing thirteen games for the Red Wings and Coach Larry Wilson. Larson played for a number of coaches in the NHL in his long career and says that Brooks, his college coach, was "by far the best coach…with great motivation, skills training, and adapting other styles and strategies." Russ Anderson played two seasons for Herb Brooks at the University of Minnesota and then went to the Penguins.

The NHL drafted nine of these eleven players over a ten-year span from 1972 to 1982. Being picked so high and then proving to be successful, these nine players established a precedent for NHL general managers and coaches to pick Minnesota players for years to come. In the first two decades of the twenty-first century, Minnesota players continued to be drafted early. The seventeenth overall pick in 2003 went to Zach Parise, and Blake Wheeler went fifth overall in 2004. The twenty-fourth overall pick in 2005 was T.J. Oshie. Erik Johnson was picked first in 2006, and Kyle Okposo was seventh overall in 2006.

Prior to this period, there had been almost no Minnesota players in the NHL, and now there were thirty in one season. For eighteen seasons (1950–51 to 1968–69), Tommy Williams from Duluth Central played for thirteen seasons beginning in 1961 (for many of those seasons, he was the only American player in the NHL) and Ken Yackel from St. Paul Humboldt played six games. From 1930–31 to 1949–50, there were eight Minnesota players. The NHL amateur draft began in 1963 with few selections: 21 in 1963, 24 in 1964, 11 in 1965, 24 in 1966, 17 in 1967, 24 in 1968 and 84 in 1969. No Minnesota players were taken for the first six years. Then, in 1969, Wally Olds from Warroad was selected 57th overall. In 1971, a number of Minnesota players were selected, led by Henry Boucha from Warroad at

MINNESOTA TALENT IN THE NHL DRAFT

Bill Nyrop – 66th overall in 1972 by the Montreal Canadiens

Dave Langevin – 112th overall in 1974 by the New York Islanders

Russ Anderson – 31st overall in 1975 by the Pittsburgh Penguins

Don Jackson – 39th overall in 1976 by the Minnesota North Stars

Reed Larson – 22nd overall in 1976 by the Detroit Red Wings

Jim Korn – 73rd overall in 1977 by the Detroit Red Wings

Mike Ramsey – 11th overall in 1979 by the Buffalo Sabres

Tom Kurvers – 145th overall in 1981 by the Montreal Canadiens

Jim Johnson – undrafted, signed in 1985 by the Pittsburgh Penguins

Chris Dahlquist – undrafted, signed in 1985 by the Pittsburgh Penguins

Phil Housley – 6th overall in 1982 by the Buffalo Sabres

16th overall, Mike Antonovich from Coleraine at 113th overall and others. Now as part of this movement with Nyrop, the highest echelons of hockey evaluation picked Minnesota players, and this was followed up within a few years by the proven success of their play. This was a paradigm shift. During this time, Reed Larson made an immediate impact after joining the Red Wings for the 1976–77 season and being an All-Star in his first full season in 1978. The next big impact player to the league from this group was Mike Ramsey, who joined the Sabres in 1980 following the Olympics and was an All-Star in his second season and in three of the next four years. Larson and Ramsey had become stars of the league. In the early 1980s, Langevin made big contributions to the New York Islanders, winning four consecutive Stanley Cups beginning in 1980.

In 1972, when Pollock and Coach Scotty Bowman made the Nyrop pick, they were at the top of the hockey world. Pollock had been general manager of the Canadiens since 1964 and had won five Stanley Cups. The other big factor with the 1972 Nyrop draft and the 1974 Langevin draft was the timing, as it was five years after the expansion draft of 1967 from the "Original Six" NHL teams and seven years after expansion took effect. In the first few years after expansion, the new teams made adjustments, bringing in a number of skilled players from the minor leagues and signing older players, some from out of retirement, from the Original Six teams in order to continue building competitive teams. After the 1972 draft, Pollock and Bowman won another Stanley Cup with the Canadiens the next year. Pollock would go on to win nine championships in his fourteen years as general manager of the Canadiens.

Amazingly, three of these nine players were drafted by the same man: Scotty Bowman. No NHL coach comes close to Bowman's 1,248 regular-season wins, 223 Stanley Cup playoff wins and nine Stanley Cup titles. Joel Quenneville is second with 282 fewer wins, which is 77 percent of Bowman's total. Bowman has a 65.7 winning percentage. No coach among the next twenty comes within 5 percent of his rate.[20]

Scotty Bowman in 2006. The greatest NHL coach played a key part for many Minnesota hockey greats, including the drafts and coaching of Bill Nyrop, Phil Housley and Mike Ramsey. Bowman has the most Stanley Cups, most wins and best winning percentage of all coaches. *Wikimedia Commons, user Arnold C.*

At the time of the 1979 draft of Mike Ramsey, Bowman had won five more Stanley Cups (1973, 1976, 1977, 1978 and 1979). In 1979 and 1982 with Ramsey and Housley, no coach or general manager at that time was more successful and more revered than Bowman, and he chose with his first pick in two of those three years Minnesota players. These decisions were watched closely by the other twenty-one teams. Bowman's decision was reinforced from the very beginning, as Ramsey and Housley became stalwarts of the Sabres and the league and All-Stars within the first two seasons.

The decision to pick Housley so high is even more remarkable because Housley had played only to the high school level. Even more remarkable, Bowman planned for Housley to play immediately. Housley went to training camp out of high school, made the team and played in the first game. Ramsey took a bit of a longer route to the NHL. He followed one year of college with the Olympics and then went to the NHL. Broten had three years between high school and the NHL with the North Stars in 1981. In this span, he was part of the 1978–79 University of Minnesota championship team with Coach Brooks and an Olympic gold medal winner in 1980, and he had another college hockey season with the University of Minnesota under Coach Buetow, during which he won the Hobey Baker Award.

Bowman gives all the credit for drafting Nyrop to Ronnie Caron, the head scout for the Canadiens. Later in the 1970s, Caron became the Canadiens'

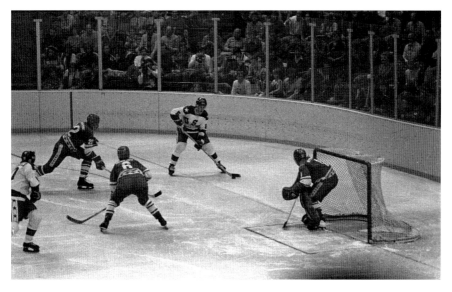

USA versus the Soviet Union at the 1980 Winter Olympics. Mike Ramsey (5) has the puck. Ramsey (Minneapolis-Roosevelt, 1984) was a four-time All-Star over eighteen seasons and 1,070 games played. *Henry Zbyszynski, Wikimedia Commons.*

assistant general manager, and he went on to be general manager of the Blues from 1983 to 1994, bringing in players such as Doug Gilmour, Brett Hull and Adam Oates. Caron was a graduate of the University of Ottawa and began his career as a part-time scout with the Montreal Junior Canadiens in 1959.

In drafting Mike Ramsey in 1979, Bowman credits the draft being postponed about two months to August 9. This allowed him to watch Ramsey at the final 1980 Olympic tryouts at the end of July in Colorado. Otherwise, Bowman would not have selected him. It was moved in 1979 because of the NHL-WHA merger. The minimum age for players was also lowered that year, from twenty to nineteen, with underage players from the WHA excepted. Ramsey was eighteen years old at the time and would be turning nineteen on December 3. In the 1979–80 season, he would play for the U.S. Olympic team as the youngest player, then go immediately to the Sabres. This was Bowman's first draft as Buffalo general manager and the first time acting as general manager in eight years since serving in that role with the Blues from 1967 to 1971. When Bowman moved to coach other teams, Ramsey would follow as his contract allowed, to the Penguins and then to the Red Wings.

This 1979 draft was incredible in many ways, in addition to being the first draft after the NHL-WHA merger. One interesting aspect of the draft was the negotiations between the NHL and Gretzky and the Oilers that resulted in Gretzky being given an exception and being allowed to remain with the Oilers and not be part of the draft. Another part of the story of the draft was the players taken before and after Ramsey who went on to be All-Stars and Hall of Famers, including the following defensemen taken before Ramey:

#1 draft Rob Ramage – 1,044 games played
#4 Mike Gartner – 1,432 games played and Hall of Famer
#6 Craig Hartsburg – 570 games played in NHL and 77 in WHA (647 total)
#7 Keith Brown – 876 games played
#8 Ray Bourque – 1,612 games played and Hall of Famer
#11 Mike Ramsey – 1,070 games played and four-time All-Star

In later rounds, three forwards, all Hall of Famers, would be drafted: Mark Messier, Glen Anderson, and Guy Carbonneau.

FOR THE HOUSLEY DRAFT in 1982, Bowman credits scout Rudy Migay, who had been big on Housley for a couple of years. Migay had an accomplished career as a player. He brought a gritty style of play to ten NHL seasons for the Maple Leafs. He then coached in the minor leagues for six seasons and scouted for the Penguins and the Sabres based out of Thunder Bay. Bowman said, "Migay played a big role in helping the Sabres find some of the best talent the hockey world had to offer drafting Housley, Barrasso, Adreychuk, Creighton, Tucker Turgeon Mogilny and many more."[21]

Migay told Bowman he had to see this kid, and Bowman came to the St. Paul Civic Center to watch Housley play for South St. Paul High School in the Minnesota State High School Tournament in March 1981, Housley's junior year. Bowman said that Housley "played the whole game moving from defense to forward and back. His skating, and puck carrying was phenomenal." The next season, 1981–82, Migay continued to follow Housley and sent glowing reports to Bowman of Housley's skating, puck-handling and scoring. He even mentioned taking Housley high in the first round and having him play with no minor-league, college or junior experience. Extraordinary scouting reports were also coming to Bowman from Ted Hampson, a former North Star and Fighting Saints player. Hampson had a direct connection with Minnesota high school hockey. His sons Scott and Greg played for Coach Ikola on the Edina East High team that won the

1978 state tournament. Greg also played on the 1979 championship team, just two to three years before Housley.

The reports from Hampson and Migay said Housley was really coming along. Bowman wanted to see Housley one more time before the draft, especially with the plan of taking him so high and making the step directly to the NHL. Bowman was planning to watch Housley at the state tournament, but South St. Paul did not make the tournament in 1982. Housley's high school hockey season was over. Housley played for the St. Paul Vulcans junior team for several weeks when the high school season was over. The Vulcans were coached by Frank Zywiec, older brother of Joe Zywiec of Sibley High. Migay was trying to arrange for Bowman to see Housley play. The Vulcans were playing their last game on a Monday evening in late March. The Sabres had the night off, so Bowman flew out from New York and met up with Rudy, and they traveled through the streets of Minneapolis to Riverside Avenue to what Bowman described as "a small, dark, arena," Augsburg College Ice Arena, then the home rink of the Vulcans. Bowman tells the story that they got in their seats and watched the first five minutes of the game and watched Housley skate "a rush like Booby Orr and I said, 'Rudy we do not have to see him anymore', and we left the game." Bowman said the Sabres "needed to build up our defense" and that Housley would be a great fit to do that. Housley was at the Montreal Forum on June 9, 1982, and Bowman selected him with the Sabres' first pick, sixth overall after defenseman Scott Stevens. This was three years after Bowman and the Sabres had selected Mike Ramsey eleventh overall with their first pick.

Housley was the highest pick of any Minnesota homegrown player and the first high school player from the state to go directly to the NHL. Bowman described Housley as a "phenom" who was "difficult to cover....He skated with such tremendous speed and power bringing the puck up on the power play and carrying the puck with no reduction in speed." Housley would have a Hall of Fame career, and it all started with those first two seasons (19 goals, 47 assists and 66 points and 31 goals, 46 assists and 77 points).

Housley attributes his immediate success in the league (other than his foundation in youth and high school hockey) to three things. First, playing for the U.S. national team in April following the Vulcans' season was a huge part of his development. Second, he says, "I worked extremely hard on my off-ice training before my first camp and knew I had to be prepared if I were to make the Sabres." Third was his teammates and his love of the game. Housley remembers making the team and the first year. "I credit a lot to the players that were on the team to help me feel comfortable when I got there.

Every game my first year was demanding and a grind, but I loved the game and practices and my teammates." For the U.S. national team, Housley's high school principal in April 1982 let him go to Germany and play in two exhibitions games with the team, after which he made the team and then played in the World Championships in Tampere and Helsinki, Finland, from April 15 to 29. This was not a national hockey team of eighteen-year-olds and under, or a junior team of twenty-year-olds and under. This was the U.S. national team. Many of his teammates were veteran NHL players. Most important for Housley's position as a defenseman, the team included Rod Langway, who played for the Montreal Canadiens for four years, winning a Stanley Cup in 1979, and was on his way to a six-time All-Star and Hall of Fame career. Ramsey experienced playing three seasons with the Sabres and was soon to be their captain. Other teammates included Gordie Roberts, Joe Micheletti, Scot Kleinendorst, Mark Johnson, Tom Gorence, Aaron Broten, Mike Antonovich, Buzz Schneider and John Harrington. The Canadian team, which the United States played, was led by Wayne Gretzky (the Oilers had lost in the playoffs), who had led the NHL in scoring that regular season with a historic 212 points from 92 goals and 120 assists. (The next player was 65 points behind Gretzky at 147 points and 28 goals behind at 64.) Gretzky was the leading scorer in the tournament. The Canadian team had a number of other NHL stars, including Bobby Clarke and Bobby Smith. Other players included Jari Kuri, Gretzky's line mate on the Oilers, playing for Finland. The Soviet team, which the U.S. team played, had Vladislav Tretiak in goal. At center was Igor Larinov, who would later go on to play fourteen seasons in the NHL, win three Stanley Cups with the Red Wings and become a Hall of Famer. On defense was Viacheslav Fetisov, who would go on to play in the NHL and win two Cups with the Red Wings. For Housley, it was a big step in his hockey development just five to six weeks from the end of his high school season. He went from playing high school kids to future NHL Hall of Famers.

In the 1983 draft, Bowman and the Sabres selected another American "pure high school" player, Tom Barrasso, a goalie from Acton-Boxborough High School in Massachusetts, with their first pick, the fifth overall. He, too, went directly to the NHL, where he had a brilliant eighteen-year career. Bowman says Barrasso "should be in the Hockey Hall of Fame."

One of the great differences among these eleven defensemen of the Circle-11D is their style of play. They range across the spectrum, from defensive defensemen to offensive defensemen to everything in between. At one end is the hard-hitting play of Dave Langevin, noted as one of a small group of the greatest defensive defensemen ever. At the other end is the charging, scoring, assisting offensive play of Phil Housley. Housley is in a very select group of the league's most offensive defensemen, with Bobby Orr, Paul Coffey, Ray Borque and Denis Potvin—all Hall of Famers. The career stats for this exclusive club are staggering:

Paul Coffey – 1,409 games, 306 goals, 1,135 assists, 1,531 points
Ray Bourque – 1,612 games, 410 goals, 1,169 assists, 1,579 points
Denis Potvin – 1,060 games, 310 goals, 742 assists, 1,052 points
Bobby Orr – 657 games, 270 goals, 645 assists, 915 points
Phil Housley – 1,495 games, 338 goals, 894 assists, 1,232 points

A more recent entrant, considered one of the greatest defensemen in NHL history, is Nicklas Lidstrom, who played twenty-one seasons, all with the Red Wings, from 1991 to 2012. He was inducted into the Hall of Fame in 2015, the same year as Housley. In 1,564 games, Lidstrom racked up 264 goals, 868 assists and 1,142 points.

Housley has more career goals than Coffey, Potvin and Orr and less than Bourque, who played 203 more games. Housley has more career assists and points than Potvin, and he played over 400 more games than Potvin. Housley in his twenty-one-season career from 1982 to 2003 has more goals assists and points than Lidstrom in 69 less games.

The other nine players of Circle-11D are spread between these two ends. Housley's first NHL game, October 6, 1982, the opener of the season following his graduation from high school, was at the Sabres' home rink, the "Aud." His coach, Scotty Bowman, had drafted him, and one of his teammates was Minnesota homegrown Mike Ramsey starting his third full season. The game was a 6–4 loss to the Quebec Nordiques, with the three Stastny brothers leading the way for the Nordiques. Housley had an assist on a power play in his very first NHL game. Housley was an immediate success on the ice. He would have seven seasons scoring 20 or more goals; in one season, he scored 31. He had six seasons with 70 or more points— more than any other Minnesota homegrown player at any position. He was selected as an All-Star seven times and is the only contemporary Minnesota player in the NHL Hall of Fame (those having played in the last seventy-two years, since 1950). In an earlier era, goalie Frank Brimsek (Eveleth, 1933) was inducted into the Hall of Fame. He played for the Boston Bruins from 1939 to 1950. Lou Nanne, who observed Housley as a general manager of a competing team for six years, described what he saw over those years as "visionary, he could see the ice well" and was "very strong offensively." He also described Housley as "an excellent creative player" and "a very gifted skater" "He was excellent on the power play," Nanne said, "and great with the puck."

The next player on the offensive end, after a sizable gap, is Reed Larson. Considered the possessor of the hardest shot in the league, Larson had a string of five seasons of 20 or more goals, one with 27 goals, and a total of six seasons of 20 or more goals and eight seasons with 60 points or more—one with 74 points. He was a four-time All-Star. Larson was the second American and first Minnesotan NHL All-Star in the contemporary period, in 1978. Nanne describes Larson an "exceptional player…[with] as hard as shot as anyone in the league…a very complete player, [who] can play defense very strong and then offensively, rush the puck and score."

Toward the middle of the spectrum is Tom Kurvers, with a style of play that led the offensive charge getting out of the zone. A Hobey Baker winner in college, Kurvers took naturally to the NHL. Next in the middle are Jim Johnson, Russ Anderson, Chris Dahlquist, Bill Nyrop and Don Jackson. On the defensive, stay-at-home end of the spectrum, next to Langevin, is Mike Ramsey. Selected as an All-Star four times, Ramsey was a big presence on teams, serving as captain for a number of seasons. Nanne describes Ramsey as "reliable, very good in the defensive zone…a defensive defenseman, a hybrid being creative with play and also very defense orientated."

The next player on the defensive end is Jim Korn. Known for his bone-crunching, legendary hits, he was a physical player for the Red Wings, Maple Leafs, Sabres and Devils. A huge presence at six feet, four inches and 220 pounds, Korn would play eleven seasons and over 597 games, collecting 1,804 penalty minutes, a Minnesota NHL career record, with the exception of Paul Holmgren, who in 19 fewer career games had 1 more penalty minute, at 1,805. When Holmgren finished playing nine seasons with the Flyers, nicknamed the "Broad Street Bullies," he had the franchise record for penalty minutes. But this is well below the career NHL record of Tiger Williams (3,966 minutes in 962 games). Basil McRae, the closest NHL player to Korn's 597 games at 576 games, amassed 2,457 penalty minutes. Korn's 1,804 penalty minutes add up to more than 30 full games in the box, or about a full season of ice time for a defenseman rotating with another pair or two of defensemen.

Langevin is known as the iconic, stay-at-home defenseman. Nanne was very familiar with Langevin's play, because he observed him for a number of years as general manager of the North Stars and especially when Nanne's

North Stars lost to Langevin's Islanders in the 1981 Stanley Cup Finals. That was Langevin's second season and second Stanley Cup with New York. Lou says Langevin was an "excellent defensive defenseman...he does not get beat...very reliable...he clears out in front and directs play." Lou says Langevin's style of play is "very much similar to the play of his coach, Al Arbour." Scotty Bowman described Arbour as coach of the Islanders as he taught defensemen on that team, such as Langevin: "With the Islanders he taught those defencemen his defence. He had been a defensive defence man, and he was a stickler on fundamentals. He would be firm, but fair. They played a regimented game in their own end."[22]

Bill Nyrop began his NHL career with the Canadiens on February 24, 1976. Nyrop would play with Montreal for the remaining 19 games of the regular season and then all of the 13 playoff games to win the Stanley Cup. That team lost only two of Nyrop's 19 regular-season games and only 1 in the playoffs. Their explosive offense was led by Guy Lafleur's 56 goals, 69 assists and 125 points. Pete Mahavolich was second in points with 105 and 34 goals; Steve Shutt scored 45 goals; and Yvon Cournoyer netted 32.[23] Nyrop joined a defensive corps with an unheard-of three Hall of Fame defensemen: Guy Lapointe, Larry Robinson and Serge Savard. "After the Big Three of Robinson, Savard, and Lapointe," says Ken Dryden in *Scotty*, "Nyrop was the fourth. Agile, and athletic, a powerful skater....With the Canadiens, he had been getting better each year, and one day he might even have turned the Big Three into the Big Four."[24] The next season's Canadians lost only 8 games, with Lafleur leading the league with 56 goals and 136 points.[25] That team had nine Hall of Famers: Robinson, Savard, Lapointe, Dryden, Lafleur, Steve Shutt, Jacque Lemaire, Bob Gainey and Cournoyer.

In these three seasons, 1975–78, with Nyrop, the Canadiens were a dominant team. They may well be the most dominating three seasons of any team in hockey or in any sport. They had just 11 losses, 8 losses and 10 losses, respectively, in each of those three regular seasons. In the playoffs, each ending with a Stanley Cup championship, Montreal had just 1 loss, 2 losses and 3 losses.[26] The strength and quality of Nyrop's play and that of his teammates is demonstrated by the second season, Nyrop's first full season. He had a plus-minus of +42, and the third season, he had an unbelievable +56.[27] No other Minnesota player has equaled that. Langevin came the closest with a +40 in 1980–81. Mike Ramsey had a +30 in 1983–85. More recently, Ryan McDonagh had a +38, his best in ten seasons. There are other examples of plus-minus stats. Hall of Famer Nicklas Lidstrom is considered one of the greatest defensemen ever. His best campaign in a career of twenty seasons, all with the Red Wings, was a +53. Defenseman Paul Coffey had one season with a +61. The record holder is Larry Robinson, Nyrop's teammate with the Canadiens, on the other defense pair. In 1976–77, he had a historic +120. He was usually paired with the high-scoring line of LaFleur, Lamaire and Shutt.[28]

KEN DRYDEN, THE MONTREAL Canadien Hall of Fame goalie who played for Bowman in their 1970s dynasty, wrote a biography of Bowman, *Scotty: A Hockey Life like No Other* (McClelland & Stewart, 2019). Woven throughout the story of the life of Coach Bowman, the NHL teams he's coached and his Stanley Cup championships is a discussion with the coach of great players and great teams. Bowman identified eight teams of particular seasons as the greatest ever. Then the book has these teams play each other—rather, each team plays as if in an eight-team tournament, the "Scotty Cup," with the winners moving to the semifinals and finals. To determine a winner for each game, Bowman weighed the strengths and weaknesses of each team during their chosen season and measured how those forces stood up against one another.

In the Scotty Cup semifinals, Bowman has this team, the 1976–77 Canadians, beating the 2001–02 Detroit Red Wings, an incredible team that Bowman coached and won a Stanley Cup with. The Wings team had nine Hall of Fame players, many near the end of their career.

In the Scotty Cup finals, the 1951–52 Red Wings face the 1976–77 Canadiens. Montreal wins and is crowned by Bowman as the greatest team ever.[29] Bill Nyrop was a contributing part of this team.

THE IDENTIFICATION OF THIS group of defensemen brings to mind other accomplished athletes from concentrated areas and times. The state of Minnesota has one of the all-time great baseball pairings in St. Paul. Paul Molitor and Dave Winfield, two Major League Baseball players with 3,000 hits, grew up within six blocks of each other. St. Paul is the only town or city in America with two such players. Both are also first-ballot baseball Hall of Famers.

For hockey, the Detroit area saw three incredible centers within about seven years. Hall of Fame center Pat LaFontaine, the third pick of the Islanders in 1983, collected 468 goals, 545 assists and 1,013 points. Hall of Fame center Mike Modano, the first overall pick of the North Stars in 1988, went on to be the greatest American scorer in NHL history with 561 goals, 813 assists and 1,374 points, second only by 17 points to Brett Hull. A third player, center Doug Weight, the thirty-fourth overall pick by the Rangers in 1990, is in the U.S. Hockey Hall of Fame. In his nineteen seasons, he played 1,238 games and collected 278 goals, 755 assists and 1,033 points.

The Circle-11D stands out for several reasons. First, there are eleven players, not two or three. Second, they did not just make the NHL and play a few seasons. They were strong NHL players, most playing more than ten seasons, one playing for twenty-one seasons. And third, they accumulated several Stanley Cups. (See Table 15: Twelve Blue Liners in the appendix.)

IN ADDITION TO THESE Circle-11D players who thrived in the NHL, the 1975–76 WHA Minnesota Fighting Saints (which played only 59 games of a 78-game season because the team went out of business) was groundbreaking for fielding eleven Minnesota players—five from the Range, four from the Minneapolis–St. Paul area, one from Warroad and one from International Falls. No other WHA or NHL team has had that many Minnesotans on one team in one season before or since. Three seasons before in the first WHA season, 1972–73, the Fighting Saints had possibly an even stronger contribution of Minnesota players, with nine solidly contributing, such as Bill Klatt, second in team goals with 36. Two goalies, Jack McCartan and Mike Curran, played 38 and 43 games, respectively. And the team played more games with five players from St. Paul or the St. Paul area and one from Robbinsdale, so six from the Twin Cities and three from the Iron Range Conference (one from Coleraine and two from International Falls). It sent a message for the start of this new league, the WHA, that Minnesota players were being selected and were contributing and leading their teams.

When Bill Nyrop began playing for the Montreal Canadiens in 1976, he got a minor penalty in one game for interference at 1:04 of the first period. Teammate Guy LeFleur got his 40th goal in the win.[30] The next night, February 25, against the Kansas City Scouts, Nyrop assisted on the game-winning goal in the third period in a 3–1 win.[31] Henry Boucha (Warroad, 1969) was playing for the Scouts after coming from the Fighting Saints. Nyrop's career was off to a great start for the nineteen games remaining in the regular season and the thirteen playoff games, ending in the Stanley Cup. None of the other Scout players in this game were Minnesota players. Nyrop was the only one on his team. On that night, February 24, 1976, the North Stars played the Islanders, losing, 7–2. For the North Stars, Pete LoPresti

(Eveleth, 1971) faced 36 shots as goalie, left-winger Steve Jensen (Armstrong, 1973) assisted on a second-period power play goal and center Dean Talafous (Hastings, 1971) assisted on a third-period power play goal.[32] These were the only three Minnesota players on the ice. The Fighting Saints had a game on February 25 against the San Diego Mariners with eight Minnesota players in the lineup. That same season, Tim Sheehy (International Falls, 1966) was in his fourth year in the WHA as a right-winger, having his best campaign, tallying 34 goals and 65 points for the Edmonton Oilers. The next season, he had 41 goals. Stan Gilbertson (Duluth, 1963) had 26 goals for the Capitals and Penguins. Mike Antonovich (Coleraine, 1969) had 25 goals with the Fighting Saints and the North Stars. The next season, he had 40 goals. Tommy Williams (Duluth Central, 1958) had 8 goals for the Capitals and the season before had 22. Bob Paradise made big contributions on defense in 57 games for the Penguins and Capitals. All of this was pioneer, groundbreaking work. Most NHL and WHA teams did not have Minnesota players that season. Even so, progress was happening in 1975–76 and in the immediate several seasons that followed, into the late 1970s and early 1980s.

4

FOUR FORWARDS AND ONE DEFENSEMAN
FROM TWO HOCKEY TOWNS

From the edge of the Canadian border, two small company towns, Roseau and Warroad, sent three players in three consecutive years to the NHL, where they each became brilliant offensive playmakers: Dave Christian, Neal Broten and Aaron Broten—a left-winger and two centers.

All three arrived in the NHL in the same twelve-year period (1970–82) as the Circle-11D players, and they are just as pioneering. These three players originated about four hundred miles to the north of the Circle-11D defensemen. In terms of time, they were around the time of Mike Ramsey's 1978 high school graduation. An additional two players, center Henry Boucha (Warroad High School, 1969), who was eight years prior to these players, and his high school teammate, Alan Hangsleben (Warroad High School, 1971), were pioneers for Minnesota players. Boucha was a pioneer in that he was the sixteenth overall draft pick in 1971 by the Detroit Red Wings. He was the team's rookie of the year in his first full season, 1972–73, but his career was cut short by an eye injury. In February 1972, Boucha went directly from scoring goals on the Olympic ice in Japan to scoring a goal in his first game for the Red Wings. Hangsleben was a trailblazer as well. After three seasons with the University of North Dakota, his pioneer period began with the WHA New England Whalers during part of the 1974–75 season and then a full 1975–76 season. He enjoyed ten strong seasons that included tenures with the Capitals and the Kings for a total of 519 games played.

Dave Christian's Team USA jersey, worn during the "Miracle on Ice" at the 1980 Olympics. Christian (Warroad, 1977) had 340 career goals, second among Minnesota players. He played fifteen seasons, 1,009 games. *Wikimedia Commons.*

Warroad, a town of about 1,800 people located seven and a half miles south of the Canadian border on the shores of Lake of the Woods, is the home of Marvin Windows. It employs about 5,500 people in the manufacturing plant, warehouse and offices, bringing employees from miles around. In addition to and part of its tradition of hockey excellence, Warroad at the time was the home of Christian Bros. Hockey Sticks, which employed about 60 people manufacturing 300,000 wooden hockey sticks a year. By the mid-1980s, that number grew to 500,000 sticks.[33] Christian Bros. Hockey Sticks was begun in 1964 by brothers Roger Christian and Bill Christian, four years after they won the gold medal in the 1960 Olympics. "Hockey Sticks by Hockey Players" was their motto. Roseau, a town of about 2,700 people, is the longtime home of Polaris, maker of snowmobiles and ATVs. It employs about 1,500 people, many of whom come from miles around. State Highway 11 connects two iconic ice arenas. Gardens Arena of Warroad opened in 1993 after Cal Marvin built the Memorial Arena in 1949. Roseau Memorial Arena, an old, wood-ceiling arena, opened in 1950. Warroad is a hockey-rich town from many angles, including being the home of more than 80 Division I men's hockey players.

In the mid- and late 1970s, Warroad was a town with deep hockey traditions. It nurtured legendary high school, college and pro players, including 1960 Olympic gold medal hockey players, brothers Bill and Roger Christian; the Marvin brothers; and Henry Boucha. Roseau was home to high school hockey powerhouses, college hockey greats and 1976 Olympic team players, including brothers John and Robbie Harris. This hockey tradition includes the legendary story of the 1960 Olympics in California. In their semifinal game, the United States trailed the USSR by a goal, and Bill Christian scored the tying goal and later took passes from his brother Roger and Tommy Williams from Duluth to score the game-winner.

These three players, Dave Christian and the two Brotens, Neal and Aaron, had a remarkable string of four hockey seasons with a mix of playing together and against one another. In the 1977–78 season, Dave Christian, in his first year with the University of North Dakota, tallied 8 goals, 16 assists and 24 points. Neal and Aaron Broten led the Roseau High team to the state tournament, where they and their teammates dazzled the crowds with Harlem Globetrotters–like passing and stick-handling, combined with ballet-type skating.

In the 1978–79 season, Christian collected 22 goals, 24 assists and 46 points. In his first year with the University of Minnesota, Neal Broten and the Gophers faced Christian in the regular season and in the NCAA Finals championship game at Olympia Stadium in Detroit on March 24. Broten scored the game-winning goal in the third period for a 4–3 win. Christian played against Coach Herb Brooks, who would be his Olympic coach the next season.

In the 1979–80 season, Christian and Broten teamed up on the 1980 U.S. Olympic team, which won the gold. Immediately following the Olympics, Christian joined the Jets in the NHL, playing fifteen regular-season games with an outstanding 8 goals, 10 assists and 18 points.

The next season, 1980–81, Christian played all 80 games with the Jets and tallied a remarkable 28 goals, 43 assists and 70 points. Aaron and Neal Broten played together on the University of Minnesota hockey team. Neal won the Hobey Baker Award as the best college player, and Aaron was the NCAA scoring champ, with 47 goals, 59 assists and 106 points in 45 games. After the college season, Neal joined the NHL North Stars, playing 3 regular-season games and 19 playoff games, including 5 games in the Stanley Cup Finals against the Islanders, who won the Cup. Aaron joined the Rockies, playing 2 regular-season games.

MINNESOTA TALENT IN THE NHL DRAFT

Henry Boucha – 16th overall in 1971 by the Detroit Red Wings
Dave Christian – 40th overall in 1979 by the Winnipeg Jets
Neal Broten – 42nd overall in 1979 by the Minnesota North Stars
Aaron Broten – 106th overall in 1980 by the Colorado Rockies

For 1981–82, Christian had 25 goals, 51 assists and 76 points and played all 80 games with the Jets. Neal Broten in his first full NHL season with the North Stars had 38 goals, 60 assists and 98 points. Aaron Broten in his first full season, with the Rockies, had 15 goals, 24 assists and 39 points in 58 games.

The drafts of these three players were within the years of the Circle-11D draft of Minnesota detailed in the previous chapter. The immediate success and great play in the NHL of these three players, especially Christian and Neal Broten, added further momentum for drafting Minnesota players.

The style of play of these four forwards was characterized by strong skating, excellent scoring, creative play and exceptional stick-handling. The centers, Neal Broten and Aaron Broten, were especially strong stick-handlers. Neal Broten and Dave Christian, both playing over 1,000 games, stand at the top of American players and the very top of Minnesota players. Neal Broten's total of 135 playoff games was at the top for Minnesota homegrown players until it was passed by Jamie Langenbrenner, who in turn was passed by Ryan McDonagh and Matt Niskanen. Neal Broten has 923 points, second only to Housley among Minnesota players and currently eleventh among American NHL career scorers—tenth if Brett Hull (whose youth hockey was in Canada) is not counted. In his first full NHL season (1981–82), Broten had 98 points; in 1985–86, he had 105 points with 61 assists, tied for ninth in scoring with Dale Hawerchuk. Neal was the first American-born NHL player to score 100 points in a season. In other eras, his 105 points would have led the league, such as in 2016–17 and 2014–15. In the 2016–17 season, the 100 points of Connor McDavid of the Oilers led the league; Sidney Crosby of the Penguins and Patrick Kane of the Blackhawks were tied at 89 points. Broten's 105-point season was from a different era of scoring. Gretzky won the scoring title that season with more than twice as many points as Broten, 215, and 74 ahead of second place, Mario Lemieux of the Penguins (141). Broten served as a captain of the North Stars and of the Dallas Stars.

Neal Broten has five seasons of 70 points or more, second only to Housley's six among Minnesota players. Broten's high quality of play was illustrated in the close-checking, high-intensity level of playoff hockey. Neal's career playoff scoring is impressive: 35 career goals, 63 assists and 98 points—the most playoff points for a Minnesota native and second only to Zach Parise in playoff goals. Neal had a monumental playoff season in 1991, all the way through to the finals with the North Stars, losing to the Penguins. He had a total of 22 points, 9 goals and 13 assists in 25 games. In Broten's fifteenth NHL season, he led the 1994–95 Devils to the Stanley Cup championship. A huge contributor, he finished third in playoff points among all players with 19, was tied for most game-winning goals with 4 and was a +13, second best in the playoffs. Twenty-two years later, in 2017, another Minnesota homegrown player, Jake Guentzel (Hill-Murray High, 2012), similarly had a remarkable Stanley Cup playoffs, leading his team to the title in his first NHL season. He led all players in the playoffs with 13 goals and 5 game-winning goals. One year later, T.J. Oshie (Warroad High, 2005) and Matt Niskanen (Virginia High, 2005) led the Washington Capitals to a championship. Oshie was part of a high-scoring offense. Teammate Alexander Ovechkin led all scorers in the playoffs, and Oshie had a remarkable 21 points, 8 goals and 13 assists in 24 games, tied for fifth overall in playoff scoring. Tied with Oshie was Jake Guentzel (Hill-Murray, 2012), playing in his second playoffs. He played in only 12 playoff games, as the Penguins lost in the second round. Guentzel had 9 goals and 12 assists and was tied at 21 points with Blake Wheeler (Breck School, 2005) of the Jets. Wheeler and the Jets lost in the third round, the conference finals. Wheeler had 3 goals and 18 assists. Along with Neal Broten leading in an earlier playoffs, these were remarkable showings in the crucible of playoff hockey, but Minnesota scoring brilliance in Stanley Cup playoffs began with Paul Holmgren (St. Paul Harding, 1972) in the 1980 playoffs, eleven years before Broten's fantastic1991 playoffs. Holmgren, with the Flyers, had 10 goals (second in the playoffs), 10 assists and 20 points in 18 games. His 1980 playoffs set the bar high at 20 points. Prior to Holmgren in 1980, no Minncsota player was anywhere near his 20 playoff points. This continued for eleven years, with no player reaching 20 points until Broten in 1991, with 22. In those eleven years, Steve Christoff with the North Stars had 12 points the same year, 1980, as Holmgren's tally. The next year, Christoff had 16 points while Holmgren had 14. Mark Pavelich with the Rangers had 9 points in 1983. Neal Broten had 10 points in 1984, and Dave Christian had 11 with the Capitals in 1988. Tom Kurvers had 16 with the Devils, and Aaron Broten also had 16 with the Devils.

LOU NANNE HAD AN up-close view of Neal Broten. Nanne was the general manager when Broten joined the North Stars and Coach Somnor at the end of the 1980–81 season for 3 regular-season games and 19 playoff games, and he continued as Broten's general manger through eight seasons. Nanne describes Neal Broten as "an exceptional talent…[with] an uncanny ability to make plays in traffic…creative…great passer…had superb balance on his skates.…He should be in the Hall of Fame."

Neal Broten and several of the Minnesota homegrown players should be in the Hall of Fame or should be given strong consideration. It is fun to compare aspects of the achievements of these players with those of players who have been inducted. For example, Neal Broten, a center, has more points and more playoff points than these three players (and possibly others) who are in the Hall of Fame: center Eric Lindros, inducted in 2016; center Peter Forsberg (2014); and right-winger Pavel Bure (2012).

Dave Christian had an incredible ten seasons of 20 goals or more, which is tied with Zach Parise as the most for a Minnesota homegrown player. In addition, he had four seasons of 30 goals or more and three seasons of 70 points or more. In the intensity of the fast-paced playoffs, Christian had 32 goals in 102 playoff games. He served as captain of the Jets in the 1982–83 season, his third full season in the league. Nanne describes Dave Christian "as unheralded with such high production…underrated…great, versatile forward, defensive play and offensive play…excellent skater."

Two years out of high school, Boucha played brilliantly for the U.S. 1972 Olympic team, winning a silver medal in Sapporo, Japan. Boucha led the team in scoring with the most goals (39) and most points (95). Nanne describes Boucha as, "Gifted. Big, strong. Excellent skater, puck handler, and shooter."

AS AN ASIDE, FOR Minnesota hockey, there are clusters of other phenomenal players who did not rise all the way to the NHL. Programs at Edina High, Hill-Murray High, Roseau High, Duluth East High, St. Paul Johnson High, Warroad High and others on the Iron Range, such as Hibbing, Eveleth, Grand Rapids and more have produced scores of Division I players.

During Head Coach Tom Saterdalen's twenty-nine-year tenure (1973–2002), Bloomington Jefferson High School produced 65 Division I players. Hill-Murray High (formerly Hill High) had more than 119 from 1965 to 2017.

One incredible cluster is the Micheletti home in Hibbing. All playing at Hibbing High, six brothers achieved a lot on the ice. Of the long, glorious history of American college hockey, which includes players from 145 teams (61 at Division I and 84 at Division III), no other brothers playing the sport come close to the Michelettis' accomplishments. The six Micheletti brothers played college hockey. Five played at Division I; the one who played for a Division III school was a two-year All-American. Tom played at Harvard University, Jerry at the Air Force Academy and Andy at Gustavus Adolphus College (Division III). Extraordinarily, three brothers over a span of eight years played brilliantly at the University of Minnesota at a high point of Gopher hockey. Defenseman Joe Micheletti (1973–77) won two NCAA championships, in 1974 and 1976. In his last year, he played with his brother, center Don Micheletti (1976–80), who was captain of the team and led that 1979 NCAA championship squad with 36 goals, 36 assists and 72 points. Center Pat Micheletti (1982–85) was All-WCHA First Team and the second-leading scorer in team history with 269 points. For the 1984–85 season, he collected 48 goals, 48 assists and 96 points. He was on the WCHA All-Decades Team for the 1980s.

There are other brothers who excelled at the University of Minnesota: from Roseau High, the aforementioned Neal Broten and his two brothers; from Richfield High, Darby Hendrickson and his brother; and from Edina High, Casey Hankinson and his two brothers. In addition, playing for the Gophers from Roseau High were John Harris and Robbie Harris, who were extraordinary college players and won NCAA championships with Coach Brooks.

Matt Cullen and his two brothers, all from Moorhead High School, played Division I hockey: Matt at St. Cloud State University, Mark at Colorado College and Joe at Colorado College.

High school hockey saw many brothers playing together, and one of the grandest were the four Peltier brothers—Skip, Ron, Doug and Bob at St. Paul Johnson High. From the 1960s to 1971, they dominated the City Conference in scoring and made many trips to the Minnesota State Tournament. Ron and Doug played college hockey at the University of Minnesota.

In addition, three brothers from the movie Slapshot, the "Hanson Brothers," were based on the three Carlson brothers, who played at Virginia High: Jack, Steve and Jeff. Jack played 508 games over eleven seasons in the NHL and WHA; Steve played over five seasons (225 games); and Jeff played 7 games. They were all six feet, three inches and weighed 205 pounds. One year separated each of them. In addition to playing together at Virginia High, all three played for the WHA Minnesota Fighting Saints in the 1975–76 season, Jack Carlson leading the way with 58 games played. (See Table 16: Four Forwards and One Defenseman from Two Hockey Towns in the appendix.)

5
GRITTY PLAYERS

First: Nine Forwards, One Defenseman and One Goalie

Around the same time that these highly touted, highly drafted Minnesotans were flourishing in the NHL, further down the draft were numerous players from the Land of 10,000 Lakes who, while not as flashy in terms of goals and points, made their mark in the league with hard-nosed, gritty play.

These players were taken between 108 to 241 overall in a draft of sixteen teams in 1972 and eighteen teams in 1974 and 1975. Tim Sheehy, Tom Younghans, Jon Casey and Joel Otto were not drafted at all. Mike Antonovich, a center out of Greenway of Coleraine High (1969), was drafted in 1971. Dean Talafous, right-winger from Hastings High (1971), was drafted in 1973. Steve Jensen, a left-winger from Robbinsdale Armstrong High (1973), was picked in 1975. Jack Carlson, a left-winger from Virginia High (1971), and Warren Miller, a right-winger from South St. Paul High (1972), were drafted in 1974, 117th and 241st overall, respectively. (In that year, Langevin was drafted 112th overall.) Also in 1974, an exception as a high draft was Gary Sargent, a defenseman from Bemidji High (1972), who was drafted 48th overall. Right-winger Paul Holmgren from St. Paul Harding (1972) was drafted in 1975 108th overall; Russ Anderson went 31st.

The style of play of these eight forwards varied greatly. On one end of the spectrum were Paul Holmgren, Jack Carlson, Sreve Jensen, Tom Younghans

MINNESOTA TALENT IN THE NHL DRAFT

Mike Antonovich – 113th overall in 1971 by the Minnesota North Stars
Dean Talafous – 53rd overall in 1973 by the Minnesota North Stars
Jack Carlson – 117th overall in 1974 by the Detroit Red Wings
Paul Holmgren – 108th overall in 1975 by the Philadelphia Flyers
Warren Miller – 241st overall in 1974 by the New York Rangers
Gary Sargent – 48th overall in 1974 by the Los Angeles Kings
Steve Jensen – 58th overall in 1975 by the Minnesota North Stars
Tom Younghans – undrafted, signed by the Minnesota North Stars in 1976
Jon Casey – undrafted, signed by the Minnesota North Stars
Joel Otto – undrafted, signed by the Calgary Flames
Tim Sheehy – undrafted, signed by the WHA New England Whalers

and Dean Talafous, relentlessly skating with hard strides and hard checks. (Holmgren added a consistent skill for scoring and assisting.) Joel Otto was similar in style to a top defensive center, Bob Gainey, shutting down and covering the other team's stars. On the other side was Mike Antonovich, flying with incredible quickness, forechecking, bugging opponents and adding goals and assists. Antonovich had seven seasons of 20 or more goals, including 40 goals in one season. In an incredible 1977–78 season for the New England Whalers, he had 32 goals, was an All-Star and led all players in goals and points in the playoffs. Similar to Antonovich was high-scoring right-winger Tim Sheehy, who had five seasons of 20 or more goals, two seasons of 30 or more goals and one season of 34. In his rookie season with the Whalers (1972–73), he had 33 goals, 38 assists and 71 points, and then he had a fantastic playoffs. Steve Jensen, a strong defensive player, showed offensive skills, with three seasons of 20 or more goals. In between was Warren Miller. Other than Otto, none of them clocked as many games as most of the eleven defensemen of Circle-11D or the Roseau and Warroad trio. Four played between 500 and 600 games. Otto is the exception, playing fourteen seasons with 943 regular-season games and 122 playoff games.

Jack Carlson played 508 games over eleven seasons (272 in the WHA, 236 in the NHL) with the Minnesota Fighting Saints, the North Stars and the Blues. He was a contributor to the North Star victories in the playoff rounds of the 1980–81 season as the team made it all the way to the Stanley Cup Finals before losing to the Islanders. Antonovich had his best season playing for the Whalers in 1977–78, with 32 goals, 35 assists and 67 points. Gary Sargent was a pioneer playing his first season with the Kings in 1975–76. A strong, sure-skating defenseman with a good degree of offense, Sargent, in his next season, had 14 goals, 40 assists and 54 points, good for fifth in scoring on the team. He was the leading scorer of the defensemen on the team that year. He was selected as an All-Star in 1980. His career was cut short by injury, but he had eight seasons and 402 games. After graduating from St. Paul Harding High, Holmgren played one year of junior hockey with the St. Paul Vulcans, then one year at the University of Minnesota. Holmgren was a contributor to the "Broad Street Bullies," the Flyers of the late 1970s. He was an All-Star in 1981 with 22 goals, and the year before (1979–80), he scored 30 goals. Holmgren would finish his NHL career with a very strong 527 games and 82 playoff games and offensive totals of 144 goals, 179 assists and 323 points. In the crucible of playoff hockey, Holmgren, in 1980 with the Flyers, had 10 goals and 10 assists for 20 points in 18 games. His 10 goals (including a hat trick) placed him second in all the playoffs. His +15 was fourth overall among playoff players.

Since his NHL career, Holmgren has had a brilliant career in coaching and administrative positions. He was head coach for eight years in the NHL, four years each with the Flyers and the Whalers. His record after 425 games was 161 wins, 219 losses and 45 ties. He then went into the front office of the Flyers as director of pro scouting, assistant general manager (for eight years), general manager (seven years) and has been president of the team since 2014. Holmgren is "Mr. Flyers" to the nth degree. Some players become head coaches and then general managers with the team they played for, but not many have done so for the length of

Paul Holmgren (*right*) in his post-playing career as president of the Philadelphia Flyers. Holmgren (St. Paul Harding, 1972) was an All-Star in 1981 with the Flyers and was a head coach in the NHL for eight seasons. *Wikimedia Commons, Author Cenpacrr.*

time Holmgren has. And no other Minnesotans come to mind. Holmgren's NHL record of games coached compares favorably to those of other Minnesota homegrown players:

Herb Brooks: 507 games over 8 seasons – Rangers (5), North Stars (1), Devils (1), Penguins (1)
Bob Johnson: 480 games over 6 seasons – Flames (5), Penguins (1)
Paul Holmgren: 425 games over 8 seasons – Flyers (4), Whalers (4)
Todd Richards: 417 games over 7 seasons – Wild (2), Blue Jackets (5)
Phil Housley: 164 games over 2 seasons – Sabres (2)

Warren Miller, right-winger from South St. Paul High (1972), graduated from high school the same year as Langevin and played four years at the University of Minnesota. Miller in 1982–83 played 56 games for the Hartford Whalers with Russ Anderson as his captain. The year before, he scored 16 goals in 74 games. Two years before that, he scored 22 goals. Miller went on to play 500 games, 262 in the NHL and 238 in the WHA.

Jon Casey, the goalie in this group, was the only player other than Mike Antonovich and Paul Holmgren to be selected as an All-Star (1993). He posted an impressive 425 games played with 170 wins, 157 losses and 55 ties. (See Table 17: Gritty Players in the appendix.)

SECOND: ELEVEN TOUGH, GRITTY, GROUNDBREAKING PIONEERS IN A SEVEN-YEAR PERIOD (1971–78): THREE DEFENSEMEN, SIX FORWARDS AND TWO GOALIES

This group of eleven players is from the seven-year period 1971–78, a span encompassing each of their first years in the WHA/NHL. This group of Minnesota greats made strong contributions to their teams in the two leagues and was a big part of the first wave of Minnesota players. But these men had short careers, ranging two full seasons to six full seasons. No player reached 500 games. They range from the two seasons of Bill Klatt and Dick Paradise to the six seasons of Stan Gilbertson. Klatt and Paradise both did pioneer work, playing the first two seasons of the Minnesota Fighting Saints (1972–73 and 1973–74), Klatt with 143 games and Paradise 144 games. Gilbertson's six seasons in the NHL resulted in 428 games played.

Mike Curran is from the Canadian border at International Falls High. Four hundred miles to the south, in the heart of St. Paul, two players came from Randolph Avenue. Tom Gorence went to school about four blocks west of Snelling Avenue at St. Paul Academy. Dick Paradise went to school about four blocks east of Snelling Avenue at Cretin High. Joe Micheletti and Mike Polich attended Hibbing High, in the heart of the Iron Range. Of these eleven players, five hailed from the Minneapolis–St. Paul area. Five played in the Iron Range Conference, four from the Range and Curran from International Falls. One, Stan Gilbertson, is from Duluth.

Four of these players played only in the NHL: Stan Gilbertson, Tom Gorence, Mike Polich and Pete LoPresti. Three men played in both the WHA and the NHL: Bill Butters, Joe Micheletti and Sreve Carlson. And four men played only in the WHA: Bill Klatt, Dick Paradise, Mike Curran and Craig Norwich.

The routes to the WHA/NHL for these players varied. Nine of the eleven played college hockey. Gilbertson and Carlson did not play college hockey. Six of the nine who played college hockey attended University of Minnesota and had brilliant college careers. Klatt, Paradise and Butters played before Coach Herb Brooks came. Polich and Gorence each won national championships with Brooks. Micheletti won two NCAA championships (1974 and 1976). Norwich played three years at the University of Wisconsin,

This group had a number of fantastic achievements in the WHA/NHL. Stan Gilbertson had 26 goals in one season playing for the Capitals and Penguins. Matt Curran, a goalie, was selected as a WHA All-Star in 1973. Bill Klatt scored 36 goals in his first season, second on his Fighting Saints team. He scored 14 goals the next season for a total of 50 goals in his first two years. In that second season of the Fighting Saints, Klatt, Dick Paradise and Mike Curran led the team with a number of other Minnesota players to a 90-point season, second in the WHA West. They went to the second round of the playoffs, losing to Gordie Howe and the Houston Aeros. Tom Gorence had 24 goals in 1980–81 for the Flyers. Joe Micheletti at defense had two seasons in a row with the Oilers scoring 14 goals. In the second season (1978–79), Micheletti, Steve Carlson (18 goals) and Wayne Gretzky, in his first season (98 points), led the Oilers to first place in the WHA. They lost in the finals of the playoffs to Bobby Hull and the Jets. Mike Polich won a Stanley Cup for the Canadiens.

FIRST SEASON PLAYED IN THE WHA/NHL

1971–72: **Stan Gilbertson** (**Duluth Central**, 1963); 6'0", 175 lbs.; left wing, 6 seasons: Golden Seals (4), Capitals (2), Penguins (2), Blues (1); 428 games played; 86 goals, 89 assists, 174 points.

1972–73: **Bill Klatt** (**Hill**, 1965); 5'11", 180 lbs.; right wing; 2 seasons: Minnesota Fighting Saints; 143 games played; 50 goals, 28 assists, 78 points.

1972–73: **Dick Paradise** (**Cretin**, 1968); 6'0", 190 lbs.; defense; 2 seasons: Minnesota Fighting Saints; 144 games played; 5 goals, 27 points.

1972–73: **Mike Curran** (**International Falls**, 1962); 5'9", 175 lbs.; goalie; 5 seasons: Minnesota Fighting Saints; 130 games played; 63 wins, 50 losses, 8 ties.

1974–75: **Bill Butters** (**White Bear Lake**, 1970); 5'10", 185 lbs.; defense; 5 seasons: Fighting Saints (3), Whalers (2), Aeros (1), North Stars (2), Oilers (1).

1974–75: **Pete LoPresti** (**Eveleth**, 1971); 6'1", 200 lbs.; goalie; 5 seasons: North Stars (5), Oilers (1); games played; 43 wins, 102 losses, 20 ties.

1975–76: **Steve Carlson** (**Eveleth**, 1973); 6'3", 190 lbs.; center; 6 seasons: Fighting Saints (2), Whalers (2), Oilers (1), Kings (1); 225 games played; 42 goals, 59 assists, 101 points.

1976–77: **Joe Micheletti** (**Hibbing**, 1973); 6'0", 194 lbs.; defense; 7 seasons: Cowboys (1), Oilers (2), Blues (3), Rockies (1); 300 games played; 42 goals, 130 assists, 172 points.

1977–78: **Mike Polich** (**Hibbing**, 1971); 5'8", 170 lbs.; center; 4 seasons: Canadians (2), North Stars (2); 226 games played; 24 goals, 29 assists, 53 points.

1977–78: **Craig Norwich** (**Edina**, 1974); 5'10", 176 lbs.; defense; 4 seasons: Stingers (2), Jets (1); 244 games played; 30 goals, 132 assists, 163 points.

1978–79: **Tom Gorence** (**St. Paul Academy**, 1975); 6'0", 190 lbs.; right wing; 6 Seasons: Flyers (5), Oilers (1); 303 games played; 58 goals, 54 assists, 112 points.

6

EARLY YEARS

PRE–GOLDEN ERA

Prior to this great flowering of homegrown Minnesota talent in the NHL, six Minnesotans in an earlier era had substantial NHL careers:

Elwyn "Doc" Romnes, center, St. Paul Mechanic Arts (1925) – 5'11", 157 lbs.
Cully Dahlstrom, center, Minneapolis South High (1930) – 5'10", 172 lbs.
Frank Brimsek, goalie, Eveleth High (1933) – 5'9", 170 lbs.
Mike Karakas, goalie, Eveleth High (1935) – 5'11", 147 lbs.
John Mariucci, defenseman, Eveleth High (1939) – 5'10", 200 lbs.
Tommy Williams, right-winger, Duluth Central High (1958) – 5'11", 180 lbs.

Between 1936 and 1944, three of these players won the Calder Trophy for rookie of the year: goalie Mike Karakas with the Blackhawks (1936), center Cully Dahlstrom, also with the Blackhawks (1938) and goalie Frank Brimsek with the Bruins (1939). Eight-time All-Star Brimsek also won the Vezina Trophy for best goalie in 1939 and 1942 and won two Stanley Cups with the Bruins. Dahlstrom and Karakas each won a Cup with the Blackhawks. In this span, Sam LoPresti played goalie for Chicago (1940–42 and 1943–44). Aldo Palazzari, a winger also from Eveleth, played 35 games for the Rangers and Bruins.

In addition to trophies, Frank Brimsek had 40 shutouts, Mike Karakas had 28 shutouts, Cully Dahlstrom had 42 points in a 44-game season and Tommy Williams had three seasons of 20 or more goals. One huge

Goalie Frank Brimsek is a member of the Hockey Hall of Fame. Brimsek (Eveleth, 1933) played ten seasons for the Boston Bruins (1938–50), was a two-time Vezina Trophy winner, an eight-time All-Star and won two Stanley Cups (1939, 1941). He led the league in wins (252) and shutouts (40). *Imperial Oil-Turofsky/Hockey Hall of Fame.*

accomplishment from this group of players is Brimsek's election to the Hockey Hall of Fame. He played with extraordinary skills for ten seasons with Boston. His nickname, "Mr. Zero," began after he recorded 6 shutouts in his first 8 NHL games with the Bruins in 1939. He continued this hot play in his first three seasons, recording 22 shutouts, more than half of his career 40 shutouts.

Right-winger Tommy Williams was a vital member of the 1960 U.S. Olympic gold medal team. He played a remarkable thirteen seasons and 802 games (663 in the NHL and 139 in the WHA). He started with eight solid seasons with Boston. He had a fantastic career record of 192 goals, 357 assists and 519 points that included three seasons of 20 or more goals and one season of 67 points.

A seventh player, Frank "Moose" Goheen (White Bear Lake High, 1915), played prior to the more organized NHL. He is in the Hockey Hall of Fame. Goheen played for the St. Paul Athletic Club, which won the MacNaughton

Trophy in the 1915–16 and 1916–17 seasons. He also played on the 1920 U.S. Olympic Team in Antwerp, Belgium, winning a silver medal.

Of note during this period is Sam LoPresti (Eveleth High, 1936). LoPresti, at five feet, ten inches and 207 pounds, played goalie for two seasons for the Chicago Blackhawks (74 games, 1940–42). On March 4, 1941, he faced 83 shots in a regulation sixty-minute game against the Bruins. Boston did not score its first goal until the 42nd shot. Though Boston won, 3–2, only 2 shots went in out of 83.

On another note, five players from the small mining town of Eveleth (population 6,887 in 1940) and from the same high school played in this six-team NHL within two years of one another.

1941–42: Sam LoPresti, Blackhawks, goalie; John Maruicci, Blackhawks, defense; Frank Brimsek, Bruins, goalie
1943–44: Aldo Palazzari, Bruins, winger; Mike Karakas, Blackhawks, goalie
1945–46: John Mariucci, Blackhawks, defense; Frank Brimsek, Bruins, goalie; and Mike Karakas, Blackhawks, goalie
Note: Some players, such as John Mariucci, left hockey to serve in the military during World War II and then returned. (See Table 18: Pre–Golden Era Players in the appendix.)

7

FIRST EIGHTEEN YEARS, NINETEEN PLAYERS

POST—GOLDEN ERA

After 1982, the next eighteen years saw twelve forwards, eight defensemen and a goalie from Minnesota who proved themselves at the NHL level.

First are four forwards, three left-wingers and a right-winger and two defensemen, all about the same size (six feet, one inch or six feet, two inches, and about two hundred pounds): Paul Ranheim (Edina High, 1984), Tom Chorske (Minneapolis Southwest High, 1985), Shjon Podein (Rochester John Marshall High, 1986), Bret Hedican (North St. Paul High School, 1988), Sean Hill (Duluth East, 1988) and Trent Klatt (Osseo High, 1989). All six players played three years of college hockey, Chorske and Klatt at the University of Minnesota. Chorske played two years there, then played a year for the U.S. national team, then went back for a third year at UM. Podein played three years at UMD. Hedican played three years at St. Cloud University. In the NHL, Klatt played twelve seasons. He played on a line of the Sedin brothers, Henrik and Daniel, for the Canucks during the brothers' first three years in the league. Podein played twelve seasons. Chorske had strong play with the Devils, scoring 21 goals in the 2003–4 season. The next year, he contributed to the team's Stanley Cup championship. After his NHL career, Klatt had incredible success coaching Minnesota high school hockey. He started at Grand Rapids High in 2015–16 and the next year coached it to a state championship.

Brett Hedican played a monumental seventeen seasons and 1,039 games. He won a Stanley Cup with the Hurricanes in 2006. He was also member of the 1992 Olympic team. A goalie, Damian Rhodes (Richfield High, 1986/Southwest Christian, 1987), played three years of college hockey at Michigan Tech (1987–90) and eleven seasons in the NHL, 309 games with the Maple Leafs, Senators and Flames. (See Table 19: Post–Golden Era Players in the appendix.)

Eight fantastic forwards followed as the first players to grow up in the post–golden era, having been bred in a hockey culture that built on the foundation of that era and added to it going forward. Eight big, strong forwards: Jason Blake and Matt Cullen from Moorhead High, Jamie Langenbrunner (Cloquet High), Craig Johnson (Hill-Murray High), Darby Hendrickson (Richfield High), Mark Parrish (Bloomington Jefferson High), Matt Hendricks (Blaine High) and Erik Rasmussen (St. Louis Park High).

Two of these players, Cullen and Hendrickson, are sons of legendary high school coaches, Terry Cullen at Moorhead High and Larry Hendrickson at Richfield High and Apple Valley High. Cullen played for his father; Hendrickson at Richfield High had Head Coach Mike Thomas. Both were from a hockey-playing family, and in each case they were the oldest of brothers who all played Division I hockey.

Their NHL accomplishments include the phenomenal achievement of 1,516 games played (first among Minnesota homegrown players) and 132 playoff games [fifth among Minnesota homegrown players] by Matt Cullen. When he ended his career in 2019, it was the most games played by an American NHL player (since passed by Hall of Famer Chris Chelios). The group also won five Stanley Cup championships, three for Cullen and two for Langenbrunner. Langenbrunner had a long career of sixteen seasons, including 146 playoff games [#2 MN], second only to Ryan McDonagh among Minnesota players, and an incredible 243 goals and 663 points. He had four seasons of 20 goals or more. Cullen and Langenbrunner top Minnesota players in NHL games played, with Cullen at 1,516, then Housley with 1,495 and Langenbrunner at 1,109. For career points, Cullen sits sixth among Minnesota players with 731, Langenbrunner eighth with 663 points. They could also score. Parrish had six seasons of 20 more goals, his highest being 30 goals. Langenbrunner had four seasons of 20 or more goals, his highest being 29 goals. Cullen had two seasons of 20 or more goals, his highest being 25. Langenbrunner was a strong leader, serving as captain of the Devils from 2007 to 2011. Parrish served as captain of the Wild. Hendrickson was known as a solid team player who played more of the defensive game with strong checking and who possessed a high hockey IQ. Craig Johnson also excelled as a great defensive forward with strong checking.

MINNESOTA TALENT IN THE NHL DRAFT

Craig Johnson – 33rd overall in 1990 by the St. Louis Blues
Darby Hendrickson – 73rd overall in 1990 by the Toronto Maple Leafs
Jason Blake – undrafted, signed as a free agent in 1999 by the Los Angeles Kings
Jamie Langenbrunner – 35th overall in 1993 by the Dallas Stars
Matt Cullen – 35th overall in 1996 by the Anaheim Ducks
Erik Rasmussen – 7th overall in 1996 by the Buffalo Sabres
Mark Parrish – 79th overall in 1996 by the Colorado Avalanche
Matt Hendricks – 131st overall in 2000 draft by the Colorado Avalanche

Rasmussen was drafted very high at seventh overall, the second-highest Minnesota player after Housley (sixth) at that time. There were strong picks high in the second round for three of the players and again later— Hendrickson at seventy-third and Parrish at seventy-ninth, with Blake undrafted. Craig Johnson's draft and selection by St. Louis general manager Ron Caron two years earlier (Caron also selected Bret Hedican) is connected to the 1972 draft of Bill Nyrop and the start of the draft of Minnesota players. Caron was the scout pushing for Nyrop's selection for the Montreal Canadiens by their general manager, Sam Pollock.

The route to the NHL was traditional for all seven players. They all contributed to their high school teams, playing all through their high school senior years. There were some differences after high school, with four of them playing college hockey for at least two years and one player, Langenbrunner, playing no college hockey, instead playing two years of junior hockey with the Peterborough Petes and then going to the NHL. Johnson and Hendrickson were teammates at the University of Minnesota for two years and teammates on the 1994 U.S. Olympic team. Parrish and Cullen were teammates for two years at St. Cloud State University. Following high school, Blake played two years of junior hockey in Waterloo then played one year at Ferris State and one at the University of North Dakota.

The style of play varied among these players, but there was a common theme of a hard-checking, huge effort and team play. Blake had one 40-goal season, five seasons of 20 or more goals and was an All-Star in 2007. Cullen did everything. He played be on penalty-killing shifts and on checking lines and then assisted on goals (461 career assists), all of which contributed to winning a Stanley Cup in his first year with the Hurricanes. There is a

The following five defensemen were about the same size and played the same position, all in a rugged, stay-at-home style: Jordan Leopold of Robbinsdale Armstrong High (1997), Paul Martin of Elk River High (2000), Mark Stuart of Rochester Lourdes High (2000), Tom Gilbert of Bloomington Jefferson High (2001) and Keith Ballard of Baudette High (2001).

MINNESOTA TALENT IN THE NHL

Jordan Leopold - 44th overall in 1999 by the Anaheim Ducks
Paul Martin - 62nd overall in 2000 by the New Jersey Devils
Keith Ballard - 11th overall in 2002 by the Buffalo Sabres
Tom Gilbert - 129th overall in 2002 by the Colorado Avalanche
Mark Stuart - 21st overall in 2003 by the Boston Bruins

Both Leopold and Martin played college hockey at the University of Minnesota, Leopold from 1998 to 2002, Martin from 2000 to 2003. They were teammates for two seasons and won a NCAA National Championship in 2002, when Leopold won the Hobey Baker Award as the best player in college hockey. Martin won a second NCAA National Championship the next year.

story from Cullen's youth, when he was on his tenth-grade football team, coached by Rod Thompson with Cullen playing quarterback. A day or two before the last game of the season, Cullen told Thompson that he would not be able to play. Thompson asked Cullen why. He said he had a hockey captain's practice. Thompson told him, "Matt, you are never going to play professional hockey." On a summer morning in 2019, Thompson watched ESPN and saw the news that Cullen was retiring after a twenty-two-season NHL career spanning 1,516 games and three Stanley Cups. Thompson's words to Cullen were either great motivation to Cullen or bad advice.

Two legendary Minnesota high school coaches, Larry Hendrickson and Terry Cullen, coached sons who became greats. Larry Hendrickson was the coach at Richfield High. He had an outgoing personality that was combined with a missionary passion for the game. He started coaching at Richfield in 1973 and took them to the Minnesota State Tournament in 1976. He started coaching at Apple Valley High in 1980 and took them to the state tournament in 1981. Hendrickson served for years as a development instructor for USA Hockey and Minnesota Hockey, running clinics, camps and coach certification clinics. Hendrickson was inducted into the Minnesota Hockey Coaches Association Hall of Fame in 2010. Terry Cullen served as head coach for twenty-one seasons, including seven at Virginia, eleven at Moorhead and short stints at Gilbert and Roseau. He was a big part of making Moorhead youth hockey a strong program, taking it to the state tournament five times, being runner-up three times and taking third place twice. Cullen was Coach of the Year in 1991 and 1992. He was inducted into the Minnesota Hockey Coaches Association Hall of Fame in 2002. (See Table 20: Minnesota Forwards in the NHL Draft and Table 21: Minnesota Defensemen in the NHL Draft in the appendix.)

8

GRAND SEVEN YEARS

Between 2002 and 2009, nineteen outstanding NHL players from Minnesota arrived in seven years, many within two or three years of one another.

David Backes, Spring Lake Park High (2002) – 6'3", 215 lbs.
Patrick Eaves, Shattuck–St. Mary's/Ann Arbor (2002) – 5'11", 203 lbs.
Zach Parise, Shattuck-St. Mary's (2003) – 5'11", 196 lbs.
Dustin Byfuglein, Roseau/Chicago Mission (2003) – 6'5", 260 lbs.
Alex Goligoski, Grand Rapids High (2004) – 5'11", 185 lbs.
Blake Wheeler, Breck School (2004) – 6'5", 225 lbs.
T.J. Oshie, Warroad High (2005) – 5'11", 195 lbs.
Matt Niskanen, Virginia High (2005) – 6'1", 203 lbs.
Justin Braun, White Bear Lake High (2005) – 6'2", 205 lbs.
Kyle Okposo, Shattuck–St. Mary's (2006) – 6'0", 220 lbs.
Erik Johnson, Academy of Holy Angels/Ann Arbor National (2006) – 6'4", 231 lbs.
Ryan McDonagh, Cretin-Derham High (2007) – 6'1", 213 lbs.
Jake Gardiner, Minnetonka High (2008) – 6'2", 203 lbs.
Justin Faulk, South St. Paul High School (2008) – 6'0", 217 lbs.
Nick Leddy, Eden Prairie High (2009) – 6'0", 191 lbs.
Derek Stepan, Shattuck-St. Mary's (2008) – 5'11", 196 lbs.
Brock Nelson, Warroad High (2009) – 6'4", 212 lbs.
Anders Lee, Edina High (2009) – 6'3", 235 lbs.

These outstanding players represent a second wave after the foundation and power of the golden era. This later era saw more arenas and a new wave of high-quality high school coaches. These years also saw the return of the NHL to the state after seven years (1993–2000) without a team. The Minnesota Wild began in 2000, when these players were in high school. The state also gained three more college hockey teams, bringing the total to five: St. Cloud State, Mankato State, Bemidji State, University of Minnesota–Duluth and Minnesota.

T.J. Oshie (Warroad, 2005) was an All-Star in 2020 and won a Stanley Cup with the Capitals in 2018. *Michael Miller, Wikimedia Commons.*

The coaching ranks included Lee Smith from Eden Prairie High, Jim O'Neil of Cretin-Derham Hall High, Curt Giles of Edina High, Ken Pauly at Minnetonka High, Wally Chapman for Breck School, Cary Eides of Warroad High, Jeff Lagoo of South St. Paul High, Keith Hendrickson for Virginia High School, Greg Trebil of Holy Angels Academy and Tom Ward at Shattuck–St. Mary's School. These men brought years of coaching and playing experience, with Edina High School probably unequalled anywhere. Curt Giles and his two assistants, Dave Langevin and Don Beaupre, bring a total of forty-three seasons of NHL experience.

The accomplishments of these eighteen players (ten forwards and eight defensemen) are many. Dustin Byfuglein was a four-time All-Star. Justin Faulk was a three-time All-Star. Two players, Blake Wheeler and Ryan McDonagh, were twice selected as All Stars. Zach Parise had ten seasons of 20 goals or more and six seasons of 30 goals or more, both Minnesota NHL records. Blake Wheeler had eight seasons of 20 goals or more and four seasons of 70 points or more. Another player, T.J. Oshie, had five seasons of 20 or more goals and 33 goals in a season. Anders Lee had five seasons of 20 or more goals, two seasons of 30 or more goals and, one year, had 40 goals. Zach Parise scored 45 goals in a season, the highest for a Minnesota NHL player and good for third in the league that season. Wheeler, with 68 assists, led the league one season, tied with another player. He had 91 points in one season, fourth among Minnesota NHL players. Several players were key parts of their team's playoff victories, including scoring clutch goals and their team winning the Stanley Cup. Several players served as captains of their teams, one for four years for one

Zach Parise (Shattuck–St. Mary's, 2003) was an All-Star in 2009. Among Minnesota-grown players, he has the most goals in a season (45), the most career goals (396) and the most career playoff goals (37). *Lorie Shaull, Creative Commons License (https://creativecommons.org/licenses/by/2.0/).*

team, Ryan McDonagh with the Rangers. Several players have been in many playoff games (160, 139, 101 and 91).

The backgrounds of these players could not be more different. Justin Faulk, Anders Lee and Alex Goligoski attended high schools with rich hockey traditions like Edina High, Grand Rapids and South St. Paul. Others hailed from schools with no state tournament appearances, such as Spring Lake Park High and Holy Angels Academy. Matt Niskanen, from the Iron Range, played for Virginia High, and Blake Wheeler took the ice for one of the state's priciest private schools, Breck School in Golden Valley.

Virtually from birth, Zach Parise was showered with pucks, sticks and skates as the son of an NHL player and director of a major hockey program, J.P. Parise. Patrick Eaves had a similar background, the son of an NHL player and coach of a hockey program, Mike Eaves. (Of the seventy-two Minnesota greats, these are the only two who are sons of NHL players.) Kyle Okposo, the son of a Nigerian immigrant, in contrast, had zero hockey background. David Backes went to a high school with no state tournament appearances, Spring Lake Park High. Grand Rapids High, where Alex Goligoski played, and Virginia High School, where Matt

Niskanen, played, each produced a 1980 gold medal team member, Bill Baker and John Harrington, respectively. T.J. Oshie was the nephew of the great Henry Boucha, who played for Warroad High School, the 1972 Olympic team, the Detroit Red Wings, the North Stars and more. Brock Nelson was a nephew of Dave Christian, who also played for Warroad High and was a key member of that 1980 Olympic team and had a long NHL career with the New York Rangers and Winnipeg Jets. Erik Johnson played for Holy Angels Academy and then the elite USA Hockey national development Ann Arbor team. Nick Leddy played for a large high school with a new, excellent program and dynasty for the previous ten years, Eden Prairie.

Curt Giles was the head coach of Anders Lee at Edina High for the three years Lee played there. Giles brought a depth of knowledge to coaching Lee from his remarkable career playing defense in the NHL for fourteen seasons, with 892 regular-season games and 105 playoff games with the North Stars, Rangers and Blues. Coach Giles's teams at Edina High have won state titles four times (2010, 2013, 2014 and 2019). Anders Lee had the benefit Giles's assistant coach, Dave Langevin, who played brilliant defense for eleven seasons in the NHL with the Oilers, Islanders and North Stars. He was a two-time All-Star with 729 games played and 110 playoff games and four Stanley Cups with the Islanders. Also on the staff was Don Beaupre, who played goalie in the NHL for eighteen seasons. He was a two-time All-Star and played in 607 regular-season games and 72 playoff games. This is a total of forty-three NHL seasons and almost 300 playoff games. There is probably no other team in the country or in Canada, Sweden or Finland, at the junior, minor-league or even professional level with a higher-credential, more-experienced coaching staff than that of Edina High School of the last eleven seasons. Their coaching style and backgrounds of defensive defensemen (Giles and Langevin) and goalie (Beaupre) are demonstrated by the play of their teams—disciplined, well-positioned, strong and defensive.

Given their varied backgrounds, these six forwards had very different routes to the NHL. David Backes and T.J. Oshie had the conventional high school hockey experience, playing their senior years at Spring Lake Park High and Warroad High, respectively. Blake Wheeler, after playing for Breck School through his junior year, spent his senior year playing for a junior team, the Green Bay Gamblers, in 2004–5. Dustin Byfuglien did not play high school hockey at all. He played youth hockey in Roseau and was academically ineligible at Roseau High School, so he played for Chicago

Mission junior hockey for a season. Zach Parise and Kyle Okposo played at Shattuck–St. Mary's School in Faribault, graduating just three years apart.

Shattuck–St. Mary's School was a hockey experience unto itself. Its program was not part of the Minnesota State High School League, as all other high school teams were, and as such was not subject to rules dictating the length of the season, number of games and other aspects. The team was not eligible for the Minnesota State High School Tournament or its playoffs. In addition, the team, organized as an AAA Midget team, did not play the high schools of Minnesota, with the exception of a game or two a season. For many years, Shattuck–St. Mary's (SSM), and Shattuck before its merger with St. Mary's, had a conventional high school hockey team playing its games against Minnesota high schools and in the private school league that included Blake School, Breck School, Minnehaha Academy and St. Paul Academy. In 1993, Shattuck–St. Mary's left the Minnesota State High School League, changed its top team from a high school team to an AAA Midget team competing on a different schedule and began recruiting students throughout the country and internationally. Even though Zach Parise, Kyle Okposo, Patrick Eaves and Derek Stepan did not have the experience of playing against high school teams, their youth hockey was in Minnesota, thus their inclusion. Okposo grew up playing in the St. Paul Harding area. Stepan grew up with Hastings youth hockey. Parise played his early hockey years in Bloomington. Eaves grew up in Faribault, playing youth hockey there before playing for Shattuck.

On a similar note, this means that Sidney Crosby, who played one year at SSM, is not considered a homegrown Minnesota hockey player, nor is Jonathan Toews, for they played just a year or two in the state and did not play pee wee, squirts or bantam in Minnesota. Patrick Eaves, who played his pee wee and bantam in Faribault and played high school at SSM, is a homegrown Minnesota player. Shattuck–St. Mary's is a hockey treasure in the state, but it is an entity largely unto itself. Greats such as Wayne Gretzky and Mario Lemieux send their sons there when they have their choice of schools in Canada or Europe. As Ken Dryden wrote in 2019 about SSM, "It is the best hockey high school in the U.S., where even Canadian kids go—including, not so many years ago, Crosby, Toews, and MacKinnon themselves."[34]

Although the high school years of these six forwards varied greatly, their draft years were similar, if not the same. Three of the six players were drafted in 2003: Backes, Parise and Byfuglien. The others followed in the next three years: Wheeler in 2004, Oshie in 2005 and Okposo in 2006.

These six players also had different routes to the NHL following their high school years. Five played college hockey; one, Dustin Byfuglein, did not, instead playing three seasons in the Western Hockey League with the Prince George Cougars from 2002 to 2005 before joining the Blackhawks organization. He played his first NHL game on November 3, 2007. Two played one year of junior hockey before college: David Backes for the Lincoln Stars of the United States Hockey League (USHL) from 2002 to 2004 and Kyle Okposo for the Des Moines Buccaneers of the USHL for the 2005–6 season. It was common for college players to play one year after high school and was recommended or "required" by college hockey coaches for most players. Three played three seasons of college hockey. Backes attended Mankato State University, now known as Minnesota State Mankato, from 2003 to 2006, then played his first NHL game for the Blues on December 19, 2006. Oshie played at the University of North Dakota from 2005 to 2008 and played his first game for the Blues on October 10, 2008, joining Backes as a teammate. Wheeler played for the University of Minnesota from 2005 to 2008 and played his first NHL game for the Bruins on October 9, 2008, the day before Oshie's first NHL game. Parise played two full seasons at the University of North Dakota (2002–4), then joined the New Jersey Devils. His first NHL game was on October 8, 2005. Okposo played a full season for the University of Minnesota (2006–7) and then played almost another half season, leaving in December 2007 to join the Islanders. He played his first NHL game on March 18, 2008.

The other ten players from the grand seven years all played college hockey. Before college, Justin Faulk and Erik Johnson played on the Ann Arbor team, Johnson for one year and Faulk for two. From 2008 to 2011, Alex Goligoski played three years for University of Minnesota, and Jake Gardiner played three years at the University of Wisconsin. Ryan McDonagh and Anders Lee played from 2010 to 2013 for University of Wisconsin and Notre Dame University, respectively. Matt Niskanen played at UMD for two years, and Derek Stepan played two years at the University Wisconsin. Brock Nelson also played two years, at the University of North Dakota. Erik Johnson and Nick Leddy each played one year at the University of Minnesota. Justin Faulk did the same at UMD.

The style of play of these players varied. Zach Parise played in front of the offensive net with grit, strength, a sense of space and movement and connections to his line mates with rebounds, tip-ins, screen scoring and setting up goals with assists. Lou Nanne describes Parise as having "a tremendous hockey career. Will not quit—talented, tenacious. Gifted as a scorer. Best

MINNESOTA TALENT IN THE NHL DRAFT

Zach Parise – 17th overall in 2003 by the New Jersey Devils
Patrick Eaves – 29th overall in 2003 by the Ottawa Senators
David Backes – 62nd overall in 2003 by the St. Louis Blues
Dustin Byfuglein – 245th overall in 2003 by the Chicago Blackhawks
Blake Wheeler – 5th overall in 2004 by the Phoenix Coyotes
Alex Goligoski – 61st overall in 2004 by the Pittsburgh Penguins
T.J. Oshie – 24th overall in 2005 by the St. Louis Blues
Matt Niskanen – 28th overall in 2005 by the Dallas Stars
Erik Johnson – 1st overall in 2006 by the St. Louis Blues
Kyle Okposo – 7th overall in 2006 by the New York Islanders
Ryan McDonagh – 12th overall in 2007 by the Montreal Canadiens
Justin Braun – 201st overall in 2007 by the San Jose Sharks
Jake Gardiner – 17th overall in 2008 by the Anaheim Ducks
Derek Stepan – 51st overall in 2008 by the New York Rangers
Nick Leddy – 16th overall in 2009 by the Minnesota Wild
Anders Lee – 152nd overall in 2009 by the New York Islanders
Brock Nelson – 30th overall in 2010 by the New York Islanders
Justin Faulk – 37th overall in 2010 the Carolina Hurricanes

deflector of pucks. Motor is always running. Zach is more talented than his father [North Star great J.P. Parise, who played 890]. J.P. was a great corner man, Zach is a scorer." In contrast, hard-charging Dustin Byfuglein and Blake Wheeler made strong shots and follow-throughs and scored with shots. Wheeler has always been a high achiever in setting up assists, leading the league in assists in the 2017–18 season. He has had a number of seasons in which he was the second-highest NHL American in points. He has had eight seasons of 20 or more goals. Of Wheeler, Nanne says, "talented, a leader of the Jets. Can handle the puck very well and shoots the puck well. Plays any kind of talent."

Speedy T.J. Oshie boasts unequaled playmaking skills and has been a scorer. Nanne describes Oshie this way: "Got everything. Every team needs such a player. Big, strong, gifted. Good hands. Uses his body well. Best shootout player." Dustin Byfuglein had a monumental playoff season to win the Stanley Cup with the Blackhawks in 2012. In a team full of scoring stars such as Patrick Kane, Jonathan Toews, Patrick Sharp (who led all players with 11 goals) and Martin Hossa, Byfuglein "led all players during the entire playoffs with five game-winning goals."[35] In the intensity of the playoffs, he rose to the occasion big-time. He was "Mr. Clutch" to the nth degree, a hero bringing a Stanley Cup to Chicago for the first time since 1961.

The defensemen are very talented players. Lou Nanne describes Ryan McDonagh as "excellent at leading the rush up ice…great playing the position…plays defense first…ability to score…great skills on the power play…leads the rush…sets up Kucherov…a big team leader, captain of the Rangers for a number of years and now an Alternate Captain with the Lightning." Nick Leddy in his very first NHL season was a steady presence on the Stanley Cup champion Blackhawks. He scored 10 or more goals in three seasons. Nanne describes Matt Niskanen this way: "Successful pro career. Very productive. Handles the puck extremely well. Sees the ice well." Justin Faulk is becoming a star of the league. He is a three-time All-Star (2015, 2016 and 2017). His offensive skills have resulted in four seasons of 10 goals or more, though he is not an offensive defenseman along the lines of Housley, Larson or Ramsey. (See Table 22: Minnesota Talent in the NHL Draft (2002–09) in the appendices.)

HIGH SCHOOL TEAMS WITH TWO OR MORE MINNESOTA HOCKEY GREATS

Games played through the 2020–21 season. *active player

Warroad (5):
- Henry Boucha, 283
- Alan Hangsleben, 519
- Dave Christian, 1,009
- *T.J. Oshie, 889
- *Brock Nelson, 666

Edina (4):
- Bill Nyrop, 207
- Craig Norwich, 244
- Paul Ranheim, 1,013
- *Anders Lee, 585

Eveleth (4):
- Frank Brimsek, 514
- Mike Karakas, 336
- John Mariucci, 223
- Pete LoPresti (goalie), 175

Shattuck–St. Mary's (4):
- *Zach Parise, 1,131
- *Kyle Okposo, 902
- *Derek Stepan, 813
- Patrick Eaves, 633

South St. Paul (3):
- Phil Housley, 1,495
- Warren Miller, 500
- *Justin Faulk, 750

Bloomington Jefferson (3):
- Tom Kurvers, 659
- Mark Parrish, 722
- Tom Gilbert, 655

Roseau (3):
- Neal Broten, 1,098
- Aaron Broten, 748
- Dustin Byfuglien, 869

Hill-Murray (3):
- Bill Klatt, 143
- Dave Langevin, 729
- Craig Johnson, 557

Virginia (3):
- Jack Carlson, 508
- Steve Carlson, 225
- Matt Niskanen, 949

Cretin (3):
- Bob Paradise, 368
- Dick Paradise, 144
- *Ryan McDonagh, 772

Minneapolis Roosevelt (2):
- Reed Larson, 904
- Mike Ramsey, 1,070

Grand Rapids (2):
- Jon Casey (goalie), 425
- *Alex Goligoski, 986

Moorhead (2):
- Jason Blake, 871
- Matt Cullen, 1,516

Elk River (2):
- Joel Otto, 943
- Paul Martin, 870

Richfield (2):
- Darby Hendrickson, 518
- Damian Rhodes (goalie), 309

Hibbing (2):
- Joe Micheletti, 300
- Mike Polich, 226

International Falls (2):
- Tim Sheehy, 460
- Mike Curran (goalie), 130

Robbinsdale Armstrong (2):
- Steve Jensen, 438
- Jordan Leopold, 695

Duluth (2):
- Tommy Williams, 803
- Stan Gilbertson, 428

White Bear Lake (2):
- Bill Butters, 289
- *Justin Braun, 772

THERE HAVE BEEN 84 players celebrated as Minnesota hockey greats in this book with brief profiles, and another 13 players are highlighted in the introduction with the vision of Dave Langevin in 1983 of the 31 players from that season. A few more are mentioned in the discussion of various concentrations of players. In addition, 101 appear in chapter 10, listing all players with 53 career points or more. Some players who are not celebrated as Minnesota hockey greats are mentioned in other outstanding records in chapter 10, such as Scott Bjugstad (scoring highest number of goals in a season with 43, second only to Zach Parise's 45), or in the same category, such as Jake Guentzel (40 goals in a season) or Mark Pavelich (37 goals in a season). Pavelich is also in the record category (two seasons with 30 or more goals and four seasons with 20 or more goals). In addition, there are players not celebrated as hockey greats who contributed to Stanley Cup championships, such as Ben Clymer and or Ryan Carter, and they are listed in the record of Stanley Cup championships in chapter 10. The 84 Minnesota hockey greats are players meeting the criterion of 500 or more games played, with the exception of pioneer players such as Bob Paradise, Tim Sheehy, Henry Boucha, Bill Nyrop, Dean Talafous, Steve Jensen, Don Jackson, Tom Younghans, Gary Sargent, 5 players from the early era and the gritty 11 pioneer players mentioned in the second part of chapter 5.

A number of great players with strong NHL careers, some with very special achievements, fall short of the standard of 500 games played and are not included as pioneer Minnesota greats. They include twenty-seven men who have played substantial seasons of NHL hockey: eight players with between 402 and 483 games played and another nineteen players with between 224 and 398 games. These players simply did not get to 500 games, requiring approximately eight to ten seasons at 50 to 82 games per season, or they did not fit into the exception category, such as a pioneer.

The nine players who saw between 402 and 483 games are (*active) *Nick Bjugstad (now over 527), Ryan Carter (473), David Maley (466), Mike Peluso (456), *Nate Schmidt (now over 517), Derek Plante (450), David Tanabe (449) and Ben Clymer (438) and Stan Gilbertson (428).

The nineteen players with between 224 and 398 games and not included are Toby Peterson (398), Lance Pitlick (393), Neil Sheehy (379), *Brady Skjei (366), T.J. Brown (365), Mark Pavelich (355), Butsy Erickson (351), Corey Millen (335), Paul Broten (322), Scott Bjugstad (317), *Jake Guentzel (300), *Tyler Ptilick (286), Chris McAlpine (282), Scot Kleinendorst (281), *Brock Boeser (253), Steve Christoff (248), Tom Pederson (240), Rob McClanahan (224) and Bill Baker (143).

The Stanley Cup playoffs have an increased intensity level, with close checking, and the entire game is played at a higher speed than in the regular season. It takes an incredible level of extra skill, grit, strength and will to perform well in the playoffs. Scoring in the playoffs, especially high scoring of goals and assists, is a measure of extraordinary achievement. But the stars have to align for a player to score a high number of goals or points in a short number of games—sometimes only eighteen, fifteen or just twelve games. The players must be performing great as a team to make the playoffs, then the team must have a hot goalie and get some lucky bounces to advance to the second and third rounds or the Finals. Phil Housley played for twenty-one seasons but had only two seasons in which his team saw 10 or more playoff games. Matt Cullen also played for twenty-one seasons and saw more playoffs and Stanley Cups, with three seasons of 24 or more playoff games and another two seasons of 10 or more playoff games.

There have been a number of seasons in which Minnesota players had exceptional playoffs, involving hot scoring and even leading or near the top of all players. Many times, they were a key part of their team winning the Stanley Cup, scoring for at least six championships. For some players, it was one very special playoffs. For others, it was a couple of playoffs with a hot scoring streak.

Total Points in Two Stanley Cup Playoffs

42 points – Jake Guentzel (Hill-Murray, 2011) was one of the very best in his very first two seasons in the NHL in the 2017 and 2018 playoffs. In 2017, he led all players in the playoffs with 13 goals, including a hat trick. He led all players with 5 game-winning goals and most even-strength goals (11). He had 21 points to lead the Penguins to the Stanley Cup. Those are amazing achievements in his very first playoffs. The next season, playing in only 12 playoff games, he had 10 goals, 11 assists and 21 points again for a total of 42 playoff points.

41 points – Neal Broten (Roseau, 1978) had two playoff seasons just four years apart, 1991 in the Finals with the North Stars and 1995 with the Devils in their Stanley Cup victory over the Red Wings, 4 games to 0. Broten had 1 point fewer than Guentzel, for a two-year playoff total of 41 points—22 points in 1991 and 19 points in 1995. In 1995, he was third overall in points and tied for most game-winning goals with 4.

35 points – Jamie Langenbrenner (Cloquet, 1993) had a phenomenal two playoffs, four years apart. He was the leader propelling his team in both playoffs to win the Stanley Cup (the Stars in 1999 and the Devils in 2003). He had 10 goals, 7 assists and 17 points for the Stars and 11 goals, 7 assists and 18 points for the Devils, a total of 35 points in two playoffs. In 2003 with the Devils, Langenbrenner led in many categories: most goals in the playoffs (11), most even-strength goals (11), tied for most game-winning goals (4) and tied for most points in the playoffs (18). The Conn Smyth Trophy should have gone to Langenbrenner in 2003, as he was the scoring leader in these categories and the Cup champion. It went to Jean-Sebastian Giguere, the goalie on the losing team. In the 1999 Stanley Cup playoffs, his 10 goals were second-best, and he was third with 3 game-winning goals. He is the only Minnesota homegrown player with two high-scoring playoffs, both ending with a Stanley Cup.

34 points – Paul Holmgren (St. Paul Harding, 1972) had a terrific run of two consecutive years of playoffs with the Flyers. In 1980, he had 10 goals, tied for second, including a hat trick. He also had 10 assists and 20 points. In 1981, in only 12 playoff games, he had 5 goals, 9 assists and 14 points for a total of 34 points in these two playoffs.

33 points – T.J. Oshie (Warroad, 2005) had two amazing consecutive playoffs with the Capitals. In 2017, he had 4 goals, 8 assists and 12 points. In 2018, he was a big part of the Stanley Cup championship, tallying 8 goals, 13 assists and 21 points (tied for fifth). He tied for the lead in power-play goals (6) and was second in game-winning goals (2).

33 points – Joel Otto (Elk River, 1981), a center, led the Calgary Flames in the 1986 Stanley Cup Finals in his first full season, collecting 5 goals, 10 assists and 14 points. In his fourth full season, 1989, he won the Stanley Cup with a fantastic 19 points on 6 goals and 13 assists (tied for fourth) in the playoffs. For both playoffs, he had a total of 33 points.

32 points – Dustin Byfuglein (Roseau) had two superb Stanley Cup playoffs eight years apart, in 2010 leading the Blackhawks to win the Cup. He had 11 goals (third best), 5 game-winning goals (first), 5 assists and 16 points. In 2018 with the Jets, he had 5 goals, 11 assists and 16 points. He had a total of 32 points in these two playoff runs.

30 points – Steve Christoff (Richfield, 1976) had a tremendous two consecutive playoff seasons with the North Stars in 1980 and 1981. For Christoff, like Jake Guentzel, these were his first two seasons in the NHL, having joined the North Stars just before the playoffs from the 1980 gold medal U.S. Olympic team. He had 8 goals and 4 assists for 12 points in the

1980 playoffs in only 12 games. In 1981, he had 8 goals and 10 assists for 18 points. He collected 30 points in those two playoffs.

30 points – Brock Nelson, in two recent playoffs, 2020 and 2021, with the Islanders has been very strong, leading his team with incredible scoring. In the 2020 playoffs, he had 9 goals, 9 assists and 18 points and 3 game-winning goals (third place). In 2021, he had 7 goals, 5 assists and 12 points for a two-year total of 30 points.

29 points – Tim Sheehy played in two consecutive playoffs for the WHA New England Whalers in his first two seasons (similar to Jake Guentzel and Steve Christoff). In 1973, he led the Whalers to the championship with 9 goals (third in the playoffs), 14 assists (also third) and an incredible 23 points (fourth in the playoffs). It was a remarkable performance for a rookie against Bobby Hull and the Jets in the Finals. In 1974, he had 4 goals, 2 assists and 6 points for a two-year total of 29 points.

27 points – Derek Stepan had two very special consecutive playoff seasons with the Rangers, first in 2014 on the way to the Finals, losing to the Kings. He had 15 points and 5 goals. In 2015, he collected 12 points and 5 goals for a two-season total of 27 points.

27 points – Matt Cullen had two playoffs eleven seasons apart, both ending with the Stanley Cup. Cullen had a tremendous playoffs with the 2006 Stanley Cup champion Carolina Hurricanes, one of his three Cups. Cullen had 18 points, 14 assists (fourth overall) and 4 goals. In 2017 with the Penguins, he had 2 goals, 7 assists and 9 points and another Cup, for a two-playoffs total of 27 points.

26 points – Ryan McDonagh at defense had two playoffs in a row for the New York Rangers in 2014 and 2017 with 4 goals, 13 assists, that was tied for 4th for most assists and 17 points, and in 2015 had 3 goals, 6 assists and 9 points for a two playoffs total of 26 points.

25 points – Mike Antonovich had two playoffs in a row, 1978 and 1979, for the New England Whalers. In 1978, the Whalers made it to the Finals. His 10 goals and 17 points led all players. The next year, he had 5 goals, 3 assists and 8 points for a two-year total of 25 points.

25 points – Zach Parise played in two playoffs with the New Jersey Devils five years apart. In 2007, he had 7 goals, 3 assists and 10 points. In 2012, he had 8 goals (tied for most), 3 on the power play, as well as 7 assists and 15 points. In the Finals, the Devils lost to the Kings, 4 games to 2.

24 points – Parise was also in two consecutive playoffs for the Minnesota Wild. In 2014, he had 4 goals and 10 assists for 14 points. The next year, he had 4 goals, 6 assists and 10 points for a two-playoff total of 24 points.

23 points – Dave Christian played in two playoffs three years apart. In 1988 with the Capitals, he had 5 goals, 6 assists and 11 points. In 1991 with the Bruins, he had 8 goals, 4 assists and 12 points for a two-playoff total of 23 points.

The 2018 playoffs featured four high-scoring players. T.J. Oshie led the Capitals to the Stanley Cup title with 21 points. Tied with him were Jake Guentzel with the Penguins and Blake Wheeler with the Jets. Dustin Byfuglein was 5 points behind with the Jets, tallying 16 points. These four players from three different teams exhibited very strong play in the same playoffs.

Three players had a string of several playoff games in six consecutive playoffs. Ryan McDonagh played 96 games with the Rangers, from the 2012 series through the 2017 series. It included the Finals in 2014, in which he played 25 games in those playoffs but didn't win the Stanley Cup. Jamie Langenbrenner had 93 games from the 1989 series through the 2003 series, the first four with the Dallas Stars. In 1999, he played 23 games and won the Stanley Cup. The next two playoffs were with the Devils, in 2003 winning the Cup in 24 games. Dave Langevin played 91 games, in each playoff through to the Finals, from 1979 to 1984. In the first Finals, with the Oilers, they lost to the Whalers. The next five were with the Islanders, the first four winning the Cup. Matt Niskanen had a stretch of six playoffs with 91 games from 2013 to 2018, ending with a Stanley Cup with the Capitals.

There have been teams with a high number of Minnesota homegrown players, including those with four or more. Some of these teams were exceptional.

The 1995 Stanley Cup champion New Jersey Devils had six Minnesota players during the shortened season. The team was one of the best, and five of these men played more than 8 games. They included the following: Neal Broten, Tom Chorske, Mike Peluso, Chris McAlpine and Ben Hankinson. Corey Millen and Ben Hankinson were not on the team for the playoffs.

The 2018 Stanley Cup champion Washington Capitals had five players: Matt Niskanen, T.J. Oshie, Aaron Ness, Travis Boyd and Shane Gersich, the last three playing eight games or fewer during the season.

The 1980–81 North Stars went to the Stanley Cup Finals with seven Minnesota players, five with a substantial number of games in the season. They were Mike Polich, Steve Christoff, Tom Younghans, Gary Sargent, Jack Carlson, Don Jackson and Neal Broten. Three of the players were from the Metro Area; four were from outside it.

The 1977–78 WHA New England Whalers had six Minnesota players. That team went to the WHA playoff finals, having finished second in the WHA with 43 wins, 31 losses and 5 ties for 93 points. All of these players had 38 games or more with the team, except one, who had 25 games. Gordie Howe led this team in scoring at age forty-nine with 34 goals, 62 assists and 96 points; second in goals with 32 was Mike Antonovich. The Minnesota players included four greats from the state. The players were Alan Hangsleben, Mike Antonovich, Jack Carlson, Tim Sheehy, Bill Butters and Steve Carlson. Four players were from the Iron Range Conference, Hangsleben was from Warroad and Butters was from the St. Paul Suburban Conference.

The 1972–73 WHA Minnesota Fighting Saints had nine Minnesota players in its first season. Besides the two goalies, all of them played 45 games or more. Five players saw 75 games or more. The nine players were Bill Klatt, Dick Paradise, Frank Sanders, Craig Faulkman, Jack McCartan, Len Lillyhom, Mike Antonovich, Keith Christiansen and Mike Curran. The first six came from the Twin Cities; the last three came from Coleraine and International Falls.

The 1973–74 WHA Minnesota Fighting Saints had six players from the state. The team finished second in the West with 90 points. The players were Mike Antonovich, Keith Christiansen, Mike Curran, Bill Klatt, Dick Paradise and Jack McCartan. Other than the two goalies, they all played 65 games or more.

The 1978–79 WHA New England Whalers had five Minnesota players, including four Minnesota greats: Mike Antonovich, Jack Carlson, Warren Miller and Alan Hangsleben. The fifth was Jim Warner. The team's record was 37 wins, 34 losses and 9 ties for 83 points, fourth in the league.

The 1978–79 WHA Edmonton Oilers, with four Minnesota players, went to the WHA finals and finished first in the league with a record of 48 wins, 30 losses and 2 ties for 98 points. The team had Joe Micheletti, Steve Carlson, Dave Langevin and Cal Sandbeck. Wayne Gretzky joined the team as a seventeen-year-old at the beginning of the season after 8 games with the Indianapolis Racers. Gretzky won the scoring title for the regular season and for the playoffs. Defenseman Langevin played in his third season and was selected as an All-Star. The playoff finals was his first of six in a row. Defenseman Micheletti was in his second season. He had

14 goals for the second year, a career highs, and 47 points. Center Carlson had 18 goals and 40 points, career highs.

The 1986–87 Sabres had five Minnesota players, including four defensemen, from Circle-11D, all on the same team. The players were Mike Ramsey, Phil Housley, Jim Korn, Tom Kurvers and right-winger Jeff Parker. They all played 52 games or more, except Parker (15 games). All five came from the Metro Area within a twenty-mile radius. Two players were from the Lake Conference (Bloomington Jefferson and Hopkins High Schools). One was from the City of Minneapolis Conference (Roosevelt High School), and two were from St. Paul Suburban (South St. Paul and White Bear Lake). Two Minnesota defense All-Stars played together: Ramsey, a four-time All-Star by this, his seventh season; and Housley, an All-Star that season and eventually a seven-time All-Star. Ramsey and Housley played together for eight seasons with the Sabres, among the few Minnesota All-Stars who played together on the same team.

The 1982–83 New York Rangers were coached by Minnesota homegrown Herb Brooks. The team had four solid players: Rob McClanahan, Mark Pavelich, Bill Baker and Scot Kleinendorst. Three were from the Iron Range Conference, of Eveleth and Grand Rapids and McClanahan was from Mounds View. The team finished with a record of 35 wins, 35 losses and 10 ties.

The 1985–86 North Stars had six Minnesota players: Scott Bjugstad, Neal Broten (All-Star), Jon Casey, Dave Langevin, David Jensen and Chris Pryor. The latter two men played 7 games or fewer in the season. The North Stars finished with a record of 38 wins, 33 losses and 9 ties for 85 points, second in the league.

The 1990–91 North Stars went to the Stanley Cup Finals with five Minnesota players: Neal Broten, Jon Casey, Sawn Chamber, Chris Dahlquist and Jim Johnson.

The 1993–94 Dallas Stars had five Minnesota players in a 97-point season (42-29-13): Neal Broten, Paul Broten, Trent Klatt, Jim Johnson and Doug Zmolek.

The 2006–7 New Jersey Devils had four solid Minnesota players in a 107-point season (49-24-9), all but one playing 72 games: Jamie Langenbrenner, Zach Parise, Paul Martin and Erik Rasmussen. Parise led the team in goals with 31 goals

The 2014–15 Minnesota Wild (46-28-8, 100 points) had seven players. John Curry, a goalie, played only 2 games. Keith Ballard saw 14 games, and Jordan Leopold, 18 games. Jordan Schroeder played 25 games.

The other players saw 53 or more games: Ryan Carter, Nate Prosser and Zach Parise.

The 2015–16 New York Islanders (45-27-10, 100 points) had four solid players, all Minnesota greats and all playing 79 games or more: Nick Leddy, Brock Nelson, Anders Lee and Kyle Okposo.

The 2017–18 Minnesota Wild had six Minnesota players in its 101-point season (45-26-11): Matt Cullen, Zach Parise, Nate Prosser, Alex Stalock, Mike Reilly and Nick Seeler.

The 2018–19 Minnesota Wild (37-36-9) had seven players from the state: Zach Parise, Nick Seeler, J.T. Brown, Matt Hendricks, Alex Stalock, Nater Prosser and Kyle Rau. Prosser and Rau played 15 games or fewer.

The 2020–21 New York Islanders (32-17-7) had four players. The team lost in the Stanley Cup semifinals, 4 games to 3, to the eventual Stanley Cup champion Lightning. The four players were Nick Leddy, Brock Nelson, Kieffer Bellows and Anders Lee.

The 2021–22 New York Islanders have four players: Anders Lee, Brock Nelson, Zach Parise and Kieffer Bellows.

ROUTE TO THE NHL

The routes to the NHL of the contemporary Minnesota hockey greats (eighty four players, less the six early-era players) were from the following colleges, or no colleges.

University of Minnesota (26)
Bill Klatt, Dick Paradise, Bill Butters, Mike Antonovich, Paul Holmgren, Mike Polich, Joe Micheletti, Tom Gorence, Reed Larson, Tom Younghans, Mike Ramsey, Neal Broten, Aaron Broten, Tom Chorske, Trent Klatt, Craig Johnson, Darby Hendrickson, Paul Martin, Jordan Leopold, Erik Rasmussen, Keith Ballard, Alex Goligoski, Erik Johnson, Blake Wheeler, Kyle Okposo, Nick Leddy

University of North Dakota (8)
Mike Curran, Alan Hangsleben, Dave Christian, Jon Casey, Jason Blake, Zach Parise, Brock Nelson, T.J. Oshie

Colorado College versus the University of Minnesota at the 2008 WCHA Men's Ice Hockey Tournament at Xcel Energy Center. Twenty Six Minnesota Greats have played for the University of Minnesota, including All-Stars Reed Larson, Mike Ramsey, Kyle Oskopo and Neal Broten. It is also where Coach Herb Brooks, a foundational figure of the golden era, won three NCAA championships in seven years. Colorado College is where Minnesota great Mark Stuart played college hockey. *Wikimedia Commons*.

University of North Dakota versus Michigan, 2011 NCAA Frozen Four event at the Xcel Energy Center. Eight Minnesota hockey greats played for UND, including All-Stars John Casey, Zach Parise and T.J. Oshie and incredible players such as Dave Christian and Brock Nelson. *Tony Webster/Wikimedia Commons*.

University of Wisconsin (8)
Dean Talafous,_Craig Norwich, Paul Ranheim, Tom Gilbert, Sean Hill, Ryan McDonagh, Jake Gardiner, Derek Stepan

University of Minnesota–Duluth (6)
Dave Langevin, Jim Johnson, Tom Kurvers, Shjon Podein, Matt Niskanen, Justin Faulk

St. Cloud State University (4)
Bret Hedican, Mark Parrish, Matt Cullen, Matt Hendricks

Notre Dame University (3)
Bill Nyrop, Don Jackson, Anders Lee

Bemidji State University (2)
Gary Sargent, Joel Otto

St. Mary's College (2)
Bob Paradise, Tom Younghans (also University of Minnesota)

Boston College (2)
Tim Sheehy, Patrick Eaves

Michigan Tech University (2)
Steve Jensen, Damian Rhodes

Mankato State University (1)
David Backes

Providence College (1)
Jim Korn

Lake Superior State University (1)
Craig Dahlquist

University of Massachusetts (1)
Justin Braun

Colorado College (1)
Mark Stuart

Denver University (1)
Pete LoPresti

No college hockey (7)
Stan Gilbertson, Henry Boucha, Jack Carlson, Steve Carlson, Phil Housley, Jamie Langenbrenner, Dustin Byfuglein

THE BREAKDOWN OF THE seventy-eight Minnesota great players by position is as follows: thirty-two defensemen, forty forwards and six goalies. The breakdown of the contemporary seventy-two players is thirty-one defensemen, thirty-seven forwards and four goalies.

Of the seventy-eight contemporary players, five held minority status: two African Americans (Dustin Byfuglein and Kyle Okposo) and three Native Americans (Henry Boucha [Ojibway], Gary Sargent [Ojibway] and T.J. Oshie [Ojibway]).

The breakdown of All-Star selections by position for the fifty-one total selections (putting aside the four Byfuglein selections, two for defense and two for forward) is as follows: twenty-six defensemen, fourteen forwards and eleven goalies. For the contemporary period's forty-three selections, twenty-nine were defensemen, twelve were forwards and two were goalies. So, in the contemporary period, defensemen make up more than twice the All-Star selections than forwards.

For All-Star selections, the figures for the defense are powered by the top seven defensemen, who were exceptionally recognized with multiple selections.

THE TRIANGLE

Six of these top seven All-Star defensemen (except Byfuglein) came from a geographic triangle measuring twelve by twelve by nineteen miles. The "All-Star Defensemen Triangle" stretches from Roosevelt High School east twelve miles to South St. Paul High School, then north twelve miles to Hill-Murray High School and then nineteen miles back to Roosevelt. The three high schools act as the three points of the triangle. Cretin High School is inside the triangle.

Triangle All-Star Defensemen
Mike Ramsey (Minneapolis Roosevelt High, 1978) (4)
Reed Larson (Minneapolis Roosevelt High, 1974) (4)
Phil Houlsey (South St. Paul High, 1984) (7)
Justin Faulk (South St. Paul High, 2008) (3)
Dave Langevin (Hill-Murray High, 1972) (2)
Ryan McDonagh (Cretin High, 2009) (2)

Triangle All-Stars Forwards
Paul Holmgrean (St. Paul Harding, 1972) (1)
Jake Guentzel (Hill-Murray, 2012) (1)
This Triangle of All-Stars at all positions includes twenty-four of the forty-one All-Star selections in the contemporary era (59 percent).

Triangle Minnesota Hockey Greats
Bob Paradise (Cretin High)
Craig Johnson (Hill-Murray)
Warren Miller (South St. Paul)
Tom Younghans (St, Agnes)
*Brett Hedican (North St. Paul) was very close, adjacent to Aldrich Arena.

Additional Triangle Strong Players
Tom Gorence (St. Paul Academy)
Bill Klatt (Hill-Murray)

Circle of All-Star Forwards from Roseau and Warroad
Neal Broten (Roseau, 1978) (2)
Dustin Byfuglein (Roseau/youth, 2003) (4)
T.J. Oshie (Warroad, 2005) (1)
*Neal Broten is the only forward or pure forward (Byfuglein was a combination) to have multiple All-Star selections (two).

From a review of the seventy-eight contemporary Minnesota great players, their teams and their conferences, a number of striking things appear. We are reminded that many teams and conferences have produced fantastic Division I and Olympic players. They have also produced players who made the NHL, including players who had strong careers but not to the level of the Minnesota greats, especially the twenty-seven players listed above.

First, there are no players among these seventy-eight from the "new" high school teams of the 1970s and the "new" hockey areas of Minnesota that did not previously have high school hockey or had very little, such as Brainerd, Detroit Lakes, Albert Lea, Austin, Red Wing, Winona, Litchfield, Alexandria, Little Falls, Willmar, Hutchinson, Buffalo, New Ulm, Mankato, St. Pater, Moose Lake and Northfield. One exception is Moorhead High with Coach Terry Cullen and Minnesota great players Matt Cullen and Jason Blake. There were players from the Twin Cities' "new" suburban schools such as Blaine (Matt Hendricks). In the next group of thirty-three players with fewer than 500 games, there were none from these "new" out-state teams. There were several from the "new" suburban schools, including Nick Bjugstad from Blaine and Tyler Pitlick from Centennial. There are many of these teams, and they have been playing high school hockey for two generations.

Second, there are so few players from the Iron Range, just eleven. Yes, the region produced players who performed at other levels, such as Division I and Olympic and, yes, at the NHL/WHA level. But these latter players played fewer games and did not attain the level of Minnesota great. For the forty years from 1982 graduation to the present, only six players came from the old Iron Range Conference teams, the traditional hockey hotbed. In first group of players, those nine who saw between 402 and 497 games, only one was from the Range, Mike Peluso from Coleraine (450 games). Two players came from the old Lake Conference (Dave Maley and Ben Clymer), two from Duluth and Cloquet (Derek Plante and Stan Gilbertson), one from St. Paul Suburban (Ryan Carter, White Bear Lake), one from Blaine (Nick Bjugstad) and one from Hill-Murray (David Tanabe). The next twenty-two players, with fewer games, include four from the Iron Range. So, in the larger group of thirty-one players listed below, of the Minnesota greats, there is a total of ten players from the Iron Range.

Third, Duluth and the Duluth greater area, including Cloquet, produced only three players over these fifty years: Sean Hill from Duluth East, Stan Gilbertson from Duluth Central and Jamie Langenbrenner from Cloquet. The next fourteen players include one from that area: Derek Plante from Cloquet.

Fourth, it was surprising that there is only one player from Bemidji, Gary Sargent. This pioneer player saw 402 games.

A review of these seventy-eight contemporary Minnesota great players shows that twenty-six are from the north part of the state (Roseau, Warroad,

Baudette, International Falls, Iron Range, Duluth and Moorhead). This area encompasses everything north of the Metro Area of Minneapolis–Saint Paul. (We can throw in Shjon Podein and Mark Stuart from Rochester.) This number, twenty-six out of seventy-eight, is about 33 percent. Over two-thirds are from the Metro Area. Of the seventy-eight players, the most recent group—those seventeen from the grand seven years of chapter 8 (graduated from high school between 2002 and 2009)—five are from outside the Metro Area (27 percent). This does not include the three Shattuck–St. Mary's players).

Longtime Minnesota hockey conventional wisdom has it that most of the best hockey talent, most of the best players and most of the strongest players in the state are from the Iron Range, the Roseau-Warroad area and the Duluth area. Many even say that the very best players come only from the Iron Range or the Roseau-Warroad area. This has been wrong for years, and it is wrong now, that "most" of the greatest players are from these northern areas. This can be refuted with one measure of the highest level of achievement in the NHL: selection to the All-Star team. The Minnesota All-Star selections are set forth in a table in chapter 10. The forty-three contemporary All-Star selections through the 2020–21 season include Neal Broten with two selections and Phil Housley with seven. Of the forty-three selections, only fourteen were from outside the Metro Area (32 percent). The thirty Metro and thirteen outside the Metro includes two players from Shattuck–St. Mary's. The thirteen selections from outside the Metro were, first, Dustin Byfuglien (4), Neal Broten (2), Jon Casey (1), Mike Curran (1), Mike Antonovich (1), T.J. Oshie (1), Gary Sargent (1), Zach Parise (1), Kyle Okposo (1) and Jason Blake (1). There are only two All-Star selections from the Iron Range or from the Duluth area, Jon Casey from Grand Rapids and Mike Antonovich. (Mike Curran from International Falls is another.) All-Star selection is only one measure, but it is an important one. Most of the All-Star selections are from the Metro area. The first nine selections following Mike Curran (WHA, 1973) include two from outside the Metro, Mike Antonovich (WHA, 1978). The others were from the Metro, beginning with Reed Larson (1978), then Dave Langevin (1979), Larson again (1980), Gary Sargent (1980), Paul Holmgren (1981), Larson (1981), Mike Ramsey (1982) and Larson (1982). Of the first twenty-six All-Star selections, twenty were from the Metro Area and six were from outside the Metro (23 percent). Yes, in the early era of the 1940s Eveleth in the Iron Range dominated Minnesota hockey, claiming most of the great players, including John Mariucci. Mariucci, the

"Godfather of Minnesota Hockey," is a foundational figure for the golden era (1960–82) that transformed Minnesota hockey. Yet the Iron Range is absent from one of the measures of great hockey achievement, All-Star selection, with the exception of Mike Anonovich.

In the foreseeable future, the northern regions are poised to be even more diminished and the Metro more prominent in terms of the origin of players achieving the level of Minnesota greatness (500 games played). Of eight identified players in the pipeline whose careers are about to reach and exceed 500 games in the next several seasons, only one is from outside the Metro Area, Nate Schmidt (St. Cloud Cathedral, 2009). These eight players are among the rising stars of the league. They include high scorers like Jake Guentzel of the Penguins (Hill-Murray High), who has played in 311 games and 51 playoff games as of November 13, 2021. Brock Boeser of the Canucks (Burnsville High) has played 253 games. On defense, Nate Schmidt of the Jets (St. Cloud Cathedral) has played 464 games and 68 playoff games. Other up-and-coming players include the following: Nick Bjugstad of the Wild (Blaine High) at 453 games, Tyler Pitlick of the Flames (Centennial High) at 386, Brady Skjei of the Hurricanes (Lakeville North) at 366, Casey Mittelstadt of the Sabres (Eden Prairie High) at 155 and Nick Seeler of the Flyers (Eden Prairie High) at 116 games.

From a review of the profiles of these eighty-four Minnesota greats in the previous chapters and from a review of the records in chapter 10 of all Minnesota homegrown players, a number of other things stand out when it comes to scoring. For scoring on defense, there are some top league achievements. For forwards with scoring, there are none to very few top achievements during the regular season. For forwards during the Stanley Cup playoffs, there have been some instances of forwards elevating their game to the very peak of league achievement.

On defense, several Minnesota players are at the top of the league in career scoring records and season records, including Phil Housley and Reed Larson, both leaders in career goals and points. Housley is at the top with several players in career power-play points and has seven seasons with 20 or more goals, one with 31 goals, and eleven seasons of 60 or more points, one with 97 points. Larson had five consecutive seasons of 20 or more goals, six seasons of 20 or more goals, and eight seasons of 60 points or more. On their teams as defensemen they have been at the top or near the top in team scoring. Housley had two seasons leading his team, the Calgary Flames, in scoring; in four seasons he was second in team scoring (three seasons with the Sabres and one with the Flames); and in seven seasons he was third in team scoring (four with the Sabres and three with the Flames). Larson with the Red Wings had two consecutive seasons ranking second in team scoring; in three seasons he was third. Several other defensemen are not at the highest level of the league or their team in scoring yet are strong offensive defensemen, including Mike Ramsey, Matt Niskanen, Alan Hangsleben and Justin Faulk.

In terms of scoring by forwards, there are no Minnesota players in the top twenty or twenty-five for career scoring (NHL career points). Neal Broten ranks 111th at 923 points, Mike Antonovich is 22nd (in the WHA) and Tim Sheehy ranks 28th (WHA). In NHL history, no Minnesota forward has won the season scoring title by goals or points. The two best seasons for the state's players were by Zach Parise in 2008–9 with the Devils, scoring 45 goals (3rd in the league) and 94 points (5th) and earning an All-Star selection; and Neal Broten in 1985–86 with the North Stars, scoring 105 points (tied for 9th in the league) and earning an All-Star selection. No other players have had seasons with higher rankings in league scoring.

In terms of team scoring, there have been many seasons with Minnesota forwards at the top of their team, sometimes as the leader in goals. Mark Pavelich with the New York Rangers in 1982–83 had 37 goals. Dave Christian led the Capitals with 83 points and had 41 goals in 1985–86. He ranked 2nd in goals (37) two seasons later. Jason Blake led the Islanders in goals (40) and scoring (69 points) in 2006–7. Derek Stepan led the Rangers in scoring in the shortened 2012–13 season with 44 points. Blake Wheeler had the most goals (28) and points (69) for the Jets in 2013–14. In four other seasons, he led the Jets in scoring, tallying 91 points in two of those campaigns. In addition, in 2014–15 he led the team in goals (26). Zach Parise was the Devils' leader in scoring and goals for three straight seasons (2007–10) and in goals for a fourth straight season. David Backes led the Blues in scoring (62 points) and goals (31) in the 2010–11 season. In the next season with the Blues, he tied with T.J. Oshie for most points and had the most goals (24). Oshie tied for the lead in goals (33) with the Capitals in 2016–17, and the season before he tied for second in goals (26).

Stanley Cup playoffs is where Minnesota forwards have achieved league records on a number of occasions, either as a scoring leader in all of the playoffs or finishing near the top of scorers, such as in the top five in goals or total points for the playoffs. In a span of forty years there have been several prime examples of this, including the amazing play of Mike Antonovich with the Whalers in the 1978 WHA playoffs. He led all players in goals and points. Jamie Langenbrenner with the 2003 Devils led all players in the playoffs in goals and in points. And Jake Guentzel with the Penguins in the 2017 Stanley Cup playoffs had the most goals of all players. In 2018, T.J. Oshie with the Capitals finished tied for fifth overall in playoff points with Jake Guentzel of the Penguins and Blake Wheeler of the Jets. Guentzel finished fourth in goals with 10.

9

FORTY YEARS AFTER THE GOLDEN ERA

From 1960 to 1982, twenty years, there was a more than 200 percent net increase in Minnesota high school hockey teams, from 75 to 154.[36] From 1982 to 2022, forty years, there was a 0 percent net increase in the number of teams. This would have been a net decrease if there had not been, in recent years, a number of new high school hockey teams, including at Holy Family High, Providence Academy and Gentry Academy.

It takes a tremendous effort to build a new hockey team. It requires many hours of work outside of practices and games. It necessitates recruiting and talking to other coaches, parents and leaders of the neighborhood, town and community. Many coaches did this work in the golden era. For example, brothers Whitey and Peter Aus built the programs of Franklin B. Kellogg High School in Roseville and Litchfield High School, respectively. Brothers Greg and Tom Vanelli coached together at St. Thomas Academy from 2003 to 2019, taking their team to five Minnesota State Tournaments, two in 1A, then moving up to 2A and taking the team to three state tournaments in that division.

The Aus brothers were unique. Both had long careers as high school coaches of programs they started—Whitey for seventeen years at Franklin B. Kellogg High and Peter for thirteen years at Litchfield High and eight years at Willmar High. Both also went on to coach college hockey—Whitey for eighteen years at St. Olaf College and Peter for twelve years at Bethel College. Both have sons who have had long careers as Minnesota high school head coaches. Whitey's son Erik Aus coached three years at Faribault High. He then was a "new program" coach for twenty-four years at Centennial High, establishing a first-class program. Peter's son David enjoyed a long career at Blaine High for fourteen years, and seven years at Brainerd High.

Whitey Aus took his Kellogg High team to the 1974 state tournament with Jim Kwapick at center leading the team. Jim played college hockey at Hamline University for Bob "Gundy" Gunderson. For Jim's last two seasons at Hamline, he played against his former high school coach, Whitey Aus, in games against St. Olaf College. In Jim's senior year (1979–80), he was the team captain of Hamline, playing with his brothers Jerry and Clemence "Junior." Gundy Gunderson was the head coach at Hamline for four seasons (1976–80), battling the MIAC teams and trying to steal a win from the Augsburg and Gustavus dynasties. For one season, he had the Kwapick brothers. Gunderson was a tough-as-nails, talented defenseman, a high school player at Richfield High (1971) with Coach Dick Bouchard. He was All-Conference for three years, battling Nyrop and Edina and the other tough Lake Conference teams. He played college hockey in the WCHA at Colorado College and was head coach at Austin High for a year before coaching at Hamline. Gundy was a class act and brought a spirit of joy and fierce competitiveness to his teams. His philosophy was that every day was a great day to play a hockey game. The high school coaching journey continued with Jerry Kwapick serving as the head high school hockey coach of the White Bear Lake girls' team for ten years (2008–19).

A common phrase in the Land of 10,000 Lakes is "Minnesota, the State of Hockey." The Minnesota Wild Hockey Club uses it on its website, advertisements and other publications. "The State of Hockey" is a trademark of the NHL's Wild and Minnesota Sports & Entertainment, which operates the Minnesota Wild. The weekly newspaper *Let's Play Hockey* and a number of youth hockey organizations also use variations of this motto. The slogan is true in many ways, yet hockey is not the most popular sport in the state, at least not at the high school level. There are over three times as many high school basketball teams as hockey teams—more than 500 to only 155. This would be similar to Indiana declaring itself "The State of Basketball" with three times as many high school hockey teams as basketball teams. However, at the NHL and NBA levels, Minnesota is more a hockey state than a basketball one as far as prominence at the pro level in terms of the number of All-Stars each year or every ten seasons, for example.

The notion that hockey is stronger in Minnesota than in any other state that may or may not be correct, depending on the factors and measurements used. If the following factors are given weight, then Minnesota is not the strongest. If they are not considered at all or not given as much weight as the number of indoor arenas, NHL roster numbers and youth registration, then Minnesota is indeed the strongest:

Massachusetts and Pennsylvania have more high school hockey teams than Minnesota: 195, 155 and 153, respectively.[37] New York has 131 and Michigan has 104. Three states have more Division I hockey teams: New York (11), Massachusetts (10) and Michigan (7). Minnesota has 6.[38]

Among leading career NHL scorers from America, Michigan has three players, Massachusetts has two and New York has two in the top ten. Minnesota has one. In terms of players among the top twenty-one scorers, Minnesota has four, Massachusetts has four and Michigan and Wisconsin have three each.[39] Incredible players from Michigan include Mike Modano, Pat LaFontaine, Mark Howe (all in the Hall of Fame) and Doug Weight. Those from Massachusetts include Jeremy Roenick, Bill Guerin, Keith Tkachuck, Tony Amonte and, early on, Robbie Ftorek, who had a brilliant WHA and, later, NHL career. Players from New York include Hall of Famer Joe Mullen and soon-to-be Hall of Famer Patrick Kane.

Another example is active NHL career scorers. There are two Wisconsin homegrown players, Joe Pavelski, and Phil Kressel ahead of all Minnesota homegrown active players.

Another example is the 2022 NHL All-Star team. Six Americans were selected, none from Minnesota and two from Michigan. Some regulars, such as Patrick Kane, were not selected. Over the last five years, since 2017, there have been Minnesota homegrown All-Stars: Blake Wheeler, Ryan McDonagh, Kyle Okposo, T.J. Oshie and Jake Guentzel.

Four other states have more NHL teams than Minnesota: New York (3), California (3), Florida (2) and Pennsylvania (2). Many hockey states have more Stanley Cups than Minnesota since the North Stars joined the league in 1967–68: New York (5), Pennsylvania (7), Michigan (4), Illinois (3), New Jersey (3) and Massachusetts (2). Minnesota has none.[40] Teams in three states have higher NHL attendance than the Wild: Chicago Blackhawks (Illinois), Detroit Red Wings (Michigan) and the Philadelphia Flyers (Pennsylvania).[41]

In most years, Minnesota has the most roster players in the league. In other years, it is close to the top. And in a few years, Minnesota is not near the top.

A new slogan is needed to motivate Minnesota hockey people toward greater goals of hockey development.

Onward with the spirit of the Minnesota homegrown greats for the incredible strength, endurance, skill, creativity, toughness and determination they have shown us. Bravo! Onward with their spirit into the future, to use their example and inspiration in order to take advantage of the deep, numerous resources of hockey intelligence, superb coaching, facilities and culture to improve hockey development for a stronger sport in Minnesota. Onward, moving up, as strong seasons continue with Jake Guentzel from Hill-Murray High and Brock Boeser from Burnsville High and others.

10

ULTIMATE LIST OF MINNESOTA RECORDS

All records that follow are through the 2020–21 NHL season.

TABLE 1
CAREER SCORING POINTS, TOP 100+ PLAYERS FROM 52 POINTS AND HIGHER
*=Active player

1,232	Phil Housley (South St. Paul, 1982)
923	Neal Broten (Roseau, 1978)
861	*Blake Wheeler (Breck, 2004)
843	*Zach Parise (Shattuck–St. Mary's, 2003)
775	Dave Christian (Warroad, 1977)
731	Matt Cullen (Moorhead, 1995)
685	Reed Larson (Mpls. Roosevelt, 1974)
663	Jamie Langenbrenner (Cloquet, 1993)
631	*T.J. Oshie (Warroad, 2005)
560	*Kyle Okposo (Shattuck–St. Mary's, 2006)
559	David Backes (Spring Lake Park, 2002)
525	Dustin Byfuglein (Roseau/Chicago Mis., 2003)

519	Tommy Williams (Duluth Central, 1958)
515	Aaron Broten (Roseau, 1979)
505	Joel Otto (Elk River, 1981)
501	*Derek Stepan (Shattuck–St. Mary's, 2008)
486	Jason Blake (Moorhead, 1992)
458	*Alex Goligoski (Grand Rapids, 2004)
421	Tom Kurvers (Bloom-Jefferson, 1980
395	Mike Antonovich (Coleraine, 1969)
387	Mark Parrish (Bloom-Jefferson, 1995)
384	*Brock Nelson (Warroad, 2009)
361	*Anders Lee (Edina, 2009)
360	Paul Ranheim (Edina, 1984)
359	*Nick Leddy (Eden Prairie, 2009)
356	Matt Niskanen (Virginia, 2003)
354	Tim Sheehy (International Falls, 1966)
345	Mike Ramsey (Mpls. Roosevelt, 1978)
340	Trent Klatt (Osseo, 1989)
334	*Justin Faulk (South St. Paul, 2008)
332	*Ryan McDonagh (Cretin-Derham, 2007)
329	Mark Pavelich (Eveleth, 1976)
328	*Jake Guentzel (Hill-Murray)
326	*Erik Johnson (Holy Angels, 2006)
323	Paul Holmgren (St. Paul–Harding, 1972)
320	Paul Martin (Elk River, 2000)

298	Sean Hill (Duluth East, 1985)
294	Bret Hedican (North St. Paul, 1988)
277	*Jake Gardiner (Minnetonka, 2008)
258	Dean Talafous (Hastings, 1971)
248	*Brock Boeser (Burnsville)
248	Derek Plante (Cloquet, 1989)
242	Patrick Eaves (Shattuck–St, Mary's)
238	Warren Miller (South St. Paul)
237	Tom Chorske (Mpls. Southwest)
235	*Nick Bjugstad (Blaine)
223	Tom Gilbert (Bloomington Jefferson, 2001)
222	Gary Sargent (Bemidji, 1972)
220	Steve Jensen (Armstrong)
214	Jordan Leopold (Armstrong)
209	Corey Millen (Cloquet)
206	Cully Dahlstrom (Mpls. South)
206	Shjon Podein (Rochester John Marshall)
205	Butsy Erickson (Roseau)
204	Elwyn "Doc" Romnes (St. Paul Mechanic Arts)
197	Dave Langevin (Hill-Murray)
197	*Justin Braun (White Bear Lake)
195	Jim Johnson (Cooper)
188	Jim Korn (Hopkins Lindbergh)
187	*Nate Schmidt (St. Cloud Cathedral)

178	Alan Hangsleben (Warroad)
175	Keith Ballard (Baudette)
174	Stan Gilbertson (Duluth)
173	Craig Johnson (Hill-Murray)
172	Joe Micheletti (Hibbing)
167	Craig Norwich (Edina)
160	Peter Moeller (Breck)
144	Scott Bjugstad (Irondale)
141	Steve Christoff (Richfield)
137	Henry Boucha (Warroad)
132	Jack Carlson (Virginia)
129	Darby Hendrickson (Richfield)
129	Ben Clymer (Bloomington Jefferson)
128	Erik Rasmussen (St. Louis Park)
124	David Maley (Edina)
123	*Brady Skjei (Lakeville North)
121	Russ Anderson (Mpls.Washburn)
116	Matt Hendricks (Blaine)
114	David Tanabe (Hill-Murray)
111	Tom Gorence (St. Paul Academy)
110	Jamie McBain (Shattuck–St. Mary's)
101	Paul Broten (Roseau)
101	Rob McClanahan (Mounds View)
93	Ryan Carter (White Bear Lake)
93	Mark Stuart (Rochester Lourdes)

90	Mike Peluso (Coleraine)
89	*Nick Jensen (Rogers)
87	*Tyler Pitlick (Centennial)
85	Tom Younghans (St. Agnes)
84	Dave Snuggerud (Hopkins)
81	Toby Peterson (Bloomington Jefferson)
80	Mike Reilly (Holy Angels)
78	Bill Klatt (Hill-Murray)
77	*Casey Mittelstadt (Eden Prairie, 2017)
72	J.T. Brown (Rosemount)
69	Tom Pederson (Bloomington Jefferson)
68	Don Jackson (Bloomington Kennedy)
65	Neil Sheehy (International Falls–Phillips, 1979)
64	Doug Zmolek (Rochester John Marshall)
63	Bill Nyrop (Edina)
62	Bob Paradise (Cretin)
62	Butch Williams (Duluth)
62	Gary Gambucci (Hibbing)
58	Scott Kleinendorst (Grand Rapids)
53	Mike Polich (Hibbing)
52	Pat Westrum (Mpls. Roosevelt)

TABLE 2
ALL-STAR SELECTIONS
(SELECTION AS AN ALL-STAR OR PLAYED IN AN ALL-STAR GAME)

8	Frank Brimsek (Eveleth High, 1933)	1939, 1940, 1941, 1942, 1943, 1946, 1947, 1948
7	Phil Housley (South St. Paul High, 1982)	1984, 1989, 1990, 1991, 1992, 1993, 2000
4	Mike Ramsey (Mpls. Roosevelt, 1978)	1982, 1983, 1985, 1986
4	Dustin Byfuglein (Roseau youth, 2003)	2011, 2012, 2015, 2016
4	Reed Larson (Mpls. Roosevelt, 1974)	1978, 1980, 1981, 1982
3	Justin Faulk (South St. Paul, 2008)	2015, 2016, 2017
2	Neal Broten (Roseau High, 1978)	1983, 1986
2	Blake Wheeler (Breck School, 2004)	2018, 2019
2	Ryan McDonagh (Cretin-Derham High, 2007)	2016, 2017
2	Dave Langevin (Hill-Murray High, 1972)	1979 WHA, 1983
1	Mike Karakas (Eveleth High, 1935)	1945
1	Mike Antonovich (Coleraine, 1969)	1978 WHA
1	Gary Sargent (Bemidji-1972)	1980
1	Paul Holmgren (St. Paul–Harding High, 1972)	1981

1	Jon Casey (Grand Rapids High, 1980)	1993
1	Mike Curran (International Falls, 1962)	1973 WHA
1	Mark Parrish (Bloomington Jefferson High, 1995)	2002
1	Jason Blake (Moorhead High, 1992)	2007
1	Zach Parise (Shattuck–St. Mary's School, 1993	2009
1	David Backes (Spring Lake Park High, 2002)	2011
1	Erik Johnson (Holy Angels, 2004)	2015
1	Kyle Okposo (Shattuck–St. Mary's School, 2006)	2017
1	T.J. Oshie (Warroad High, 2005)	2020
1	Jake Guentzel (Hill-Murray, 2012)	2020

Periods of Strong All-Star Selections in 82 Years: 1939–2021:

9 Years (1939–48): 9 All-Star Selections: all Goalie selections: Frank Brimsek (8) and Mike Karakas (1).

15 Years (1978–93) 22 All-Star Selections: 17 Defense; 4 Forwards and 1 Goalie: Defense: Phil Housley (6), Mike Ramsey (4), Reed Larson (4), Dave Langevin (2), Gary Sargent (1), Forwards: Neal Broten (2), Paul Holmgren (1), Mike Antonovich (1) and Goalie: Jon Casey (1).

14 Years (2007–21) 17 All-Star Selections: 10 Forwards and 7 Defensemen: Dustin Byfuglein (2, twice for defense and twice for forward), Blake Wheeler (2), Jason Blake (1), Zach Parise (1), David Backes (1), Kyle Okposo (1), T.J. Oshie (1) and Jake Guentzel (1); Defense: Justin Faulk (3), Dustin Byfuglein (2) and Ryan McDonagh (2).

TABLE 3
CAREER GOALS
* = active player

408	*Zach Parise (Shattuck–St. Mary's, 2003)
340	Dave Christian (Warroad, 1977)
338	Phil Housley (South St. Paul, 1982)
291	*Blake Wheeler (Breck, 2004)
289	Neal Broten (Roseau, 1978)
268	*T.J. Oshie (Warroad, 2005)
266	Matt Cullen (Moorhead, 1995)
247	David Backes (Spring Lake Park, 2002)
243	Jamie Langenbrenner (Cloquet, 1993)
222	Reed Larson (Mpls.Roosevelt, 1974)
216	Mark Parish (Bloomington Jefferson, 1995)
216	*Kyle Okposo (Shattuck–St. Mary's, 2005)
201	*Brock Nelson (Warroad, 2010)
177	Dustin Byfuglein (Roseau youth, 2003)

TABLE 4
SCORING, SEASONS WITH 20 OR MORE GOALS
* =active player

10	Dave Christian (Warroad, 1977)
10	*Zach Parise (Shattuck–St. Mary's, 2003)
8	*Blake Wheeler (Breck, 2004)
8	Phil Housley (South St. Paul, 1982)
7	Mike Antonovich (Coleraine, 1969)
6	Reed Larson (Mpls. Roosevelt, 1974)
6	David Backes (Spring Lake Park, 2002)
6	*Brock Nelson (Warroad, 2009)
6	*T.J. Oshie (Warroad, 2005)
6	*Anders Lee (Edina, 2009)
5	Neal Broten (Roseau, 1978)
5	*Jake Guentzel (Hill-Murray, 2012)
5	Jason Blake (Moorhead, 1992)
5	Tim Sheehy (International Falls, 1966)
4	Mark Pavelich (Eveleth, 1976)
4	Jamie Langenbrenner (Cloquet, 1993)
4	*Kyle Okposo (Shattuck, 2005)
4	*Brock Boeser (Burnsville, 2013)
3	Paul Ranheim (Edina, 1984)
3	Tommy Williams (Duluth Central, 1958)
3	Aaron Broten (Roseau, 1979)
3	Steve Jensen (Armstrong, 1973)

3	Tommy Williams (Duluth Central, 1958)
3	Derek Plante (Cloquet, 1989)
2	Steve Christoff (Richfield, 1976)
2	Dustin Byfuglein (Roseau, 2002)
2	Paul Holmgren (St. Paul Harding, 1973)
2	Matt Cullen (Moorhead, 1995)
2	Joel Otto (Elk River, 1981)
2	Butsy Erickson (Roseau, 1978)
2	Derek Stepan (Shattuck, 2008)
2	Patrick Eaves (Shattuck–St. Mary's, 2002)
1	Stan Gilbertson (Duluth Central, 1963)
1	Dean Talafous (Hastings, 1971)
1	Tom Gorence (St. Paul Academy, 1974)
1	Bill Klatt (Hill-Murray, 1
1	Rob McClanahan (Mounds View, 1976)
1	Peter Mueller (Breck, 2003)
1	Nick Bjugstad (Blaine, 2010)

TABLE 5
SCORING: SEASONS WITH 30 OR MORE GOALS

6	*Zach Parise (Shattuck–St. Mary's, 2003)
4	Dave Christian (Warroad, 1977)
3	Tim Sheehy (International Falls, 1966)
2	Neal Broten (Roseau, 1978)
2	David Backes (Spring Lake Park, 2002)
2	Mark Pavelich (Eveleth, 1976)
2	*Anders Lee (Edina, 2009)
2	*Jake Guentzel (Hill-Murray, 2012)
2	Mike Antonovich (Coleraine, 1969)
1	*T. J. Oshie (Warroad, 2005)
1	Phil Housley (South St. Paul, 1984)
1	Jason Blake (Moorhead, 1992)
1	Scott Bjugstad (Irondale, 1979)
1	Bill Klatt (Hill-Murray, 1965)
1	*Brock Nelson (Warroad, 2001)

TABLE 6
SCORING: MOST GOALS IN A SEASON

45	Zach Parise (Shattuck–St. Mary's)	2008–9 Devils
43	Scott Bjugstad (Irondale)	1985–86 North Stars
41	Dave Christian (Warroad)	1985–86 Capitals
41	Tim Sheehy (International Falls)	1976–77 Bulls, Oilers
40	Anders Lee (Edina)	2017–18 Islanders
40	Mike Antonovich (Coleraine)	1976–77 Oilers, Whalers, Fighting Saints
40	Jake Guentzel (Hill-Murray)	2018–19 Penguins

40	Jason Blake (Moorhead)	2006–07 Islanders
40	Jake Guentzel (Hill-Murray)	2021–22 Penguins
38	Neal Broten (Roseau)	1981–82 North Stars
38	Zach Parise (Shattuck–St. Mary's)	2009–10 Devils
37	Mark Pavelich (Eveleth)	1982–83 Rangers
37	Dave Christian (Warroad)	1987–89 Capitals
36	Bill Klatt (Hill-Murray)	1972–73 Fighting Saints
34	Anders Lee (Edina)	2016–17 Islanders
34	Tim Sheehy (International Falls)	1975–76 Oilers
34	Dave Christian (Warroad)	1988–89 Capitals
33	T.J. Oshie (Warroad)	2016–17 Capitals
33	Mark Pavelich (Eveleth)	1981–82 Rangers
33	Zach Parise (Shattuck–St. Mary's)	2014–15 Wild
33	Tim Sheehy (International Falls)	1972–73 Whalers
32	Mike Antonovich (Coleraine)	1977–78 Whalers
32	Neal Broten (Roseau)	1982–83 North Stars
32	Dave Christian (Warroad)	1990–91 Bruins
31	Phil Housley (South St. Paul)	1983–84 Sabres
31	David Backes (Spring Lake Park)	2009–10, 2010–11 Blues
30	Mark Parrish (Bloomington-Jefferson)	2001–2 Islanders
30	Paul Holmgren (St. Paul Harding)	1979–80 Flyers
29	Jamie Langenbrenner (Cloquet)	2008–9 Devils
29	Brock Boeser (Burnsville)	2017–18 Canucks

29	Phil Housley (South St. Paul)	1987–88 Sabres
28	Blake Wheeler (Breck)	2013–14 Jets
28	Jason Blake (Moorhead)	2005–6 Islanders
27	Reed Larson (Mpls. Roosevelt)	1980–81 Red Wings
27	Kyle Okposo (Shattuck–St. Mary's)	2013–14 Islanders
26	Stan Gilbertson (Duluth)	1975–76 Capitals and Penguins
26	Blake Wheeler (Breck)	2014–14, 2015–16 and 2016–17 Jets
26	Aaron Broten (Roseau)	1986–87, 1987–88 Devils
26	Brock Nelson (Warroad)	2015–16, 2019–20 Islanders
26	T.J. Oshie (Warroad)	2015–16 and 2019–20 Capitals
26	Paul Ranheim (Edina)	1989–90 Flames
26	Steve Christoff (Richfield)	1980–81 and 1981–82 North Stars
26	Warren Miller (South St. Paul)	1978–79 Whalers
26	Mark Parrish (Bloomington-Jefferson)	1999–2000 Panthers
25	Matt Cullen (Moorhead)	2005–6 Hurricanes
25	Joel Otto (Elk River)	1985–86 Flames

TABLE 7
SCORING: SEASONS WITH 60 POINTS OR MORE
*= active player

11	Phil Housley (South St. Paul)
8	Reed Larson (Mpls. Roosevelt)
8	*Zack Parise (Shattuck)
8	*Blake Wheeler (Breck)
6	Neal Broten (Roseau)
6	Dave Christian (Warroad)
4	Tim Sheehy (International Falls)
3	Jamie Langenbrenner (Cloquet)
3	Mark Pavelich (Eveleth)
2	*Kyle Okposo (Shattuck)
2	Aaron Broten (Roseau)
2	Mike Antonovich (Coleraine)
2	Jason Blake (Moorhead)
2	*Jake Guentzel (Hill-Murray)
1	Jason Blake (Moorhead)
1	David Backes (Spring Lake Park)
1	Tommy Williams (Duluth Central)
1	Mark Parrish (Bloomington Jefferson)
1	Tom Kurvers (Bloomington Jefferson)
1	*T.J. Oshie (Warroad)
1	Paul Holmgren (St. Paul Harding)
1	Scott Bjugstad (Irondale)

TABLE 8
SCORING: MOST POINTS IN A SEASON

105	Neal Broten (Roseau)	1985–86 North Stars
98	Neal Broten (Roseau)	1981–82 North Stars
97	Phil Housley (South St. Paul)	1992–93 Jets
94	Zach Parise (Shattuck–St. Mary's)	2008–9 Devils
91	Blake Wheeler (Breck)	2017–18, 2018–19 Jets
89	Neal Broten (Roseau)	1983–84 North Stars
86	Phil Housley (South St. Paul)	1991–92 Jets
85	Neal Broten (Roseau)	1989–90 North Stars
83	Dave Christian (Warroad)	1983–84 Capitals
83	Aaron Broten (Roseau)	1987–88 Devils
83	Jake Guentzel (Hill-Murray)	2021–22 Penguins
82	Mark Pavelich (Eveleth	1983–84 Rangers
82	Zach Parise (Shattuck–St.Mary's)	2009–10 Devils
81	Dave Christian (Warroad)	1983–84 Capitols
81	Phil Housley (South St. Paul)	1989–90 Sabres
79	Tim Sheehy (International Falls)	1972–73 Whalers
77	Neal Broten (Roseau)	1982–83 North Stars
77	Phil Housley (South St. Paul)	1983–84 Sabres
76	Dave Christian (Warroad)	1981–82 Jets
76	Scott Bjugstad (Irondale)	1985–86 North Stars
76	Jake Guentzel (Hill-Murray)	2018–19 Penguins
76	Mark Pavelich (Eveleth)	1981–82 Rangers
76	Phil Housley (South St. Paul)	1990–91 Jets

74	Reed Larson (Mpls.Roosevelt)	1982–83 Red Wings
71	Tim Sheehy (International Falls)	1972–73 Whalers
70	Phil Housley (South St. Paul)	1988–89 Sabres
69	Jamie Langenbrenner (Cloquet)	2008–9 Devils
69	Jason Blake (Moorhead)	2006–7 Islanders
69	Neal Broten (Roseau)	1990–91 North Stars
69	Phil Housley (South St. Paul)	1984–85 Sabres
67	Reed Larson (Mpls. Roosevelt)	1978–79 Red Wings
66	Reed Larson (Mpls. Roosevelt)	1979–80 Red Wings
62	David Backes (Spring Lake Park)	2010–11 Blues
62	Anders Lee (Edina)	2017–18 Islanders
60	T.J. Oshie (Warroad)	2013–14 Blues
56	Dustin Byfuglein (Roseau)	2013–14 Jets

Scoring Streaks
First Two Full Seasons for the Following Players (Goals)

70 – Mark Pavelich, 1981–82 and 1982–83: 33 and 37 goals (points 76 + 75 = 151)

70 – Neal Broten, 1981–82 and 1982–83: 38 and 32 goals. (points 98 + 77 = 175)

62 – Tim Sheehy, 1972–73 and 1973–74: 33 and 29 goals. (points79 + 71 = 150)

62 – Jake Guentzel, 2017–18 and 2018–19: 22 and 40 goals

55 – Brock Boeser, 2017–18 and 2018–19: 29 and 26 goals

53 – Dave Christian, 1980–81 and 1981–82: 28 and 25 goals (points 71 + 76 = 147)

52 – Steve Christoff, 1980–81 and 1981–82: 26 and 26 goals

50 – Phil Housley, 1982–83 and 1983–84: 19 and 31 goals

50 – Bill Klatt, 1972–73 and 1973–74: 36 and 14 goals

44 – Joel Otto, 1985–86 and 1986–87: 25 and 19 goals

Other Seasons Best Scoring in Two Seasons (Goals)
83 – *Zach Parise, fourth (2008–9) and fifth (2009–10) seasons, Devils, 45 and 38 goals
75 – Tim Sheehy, fourth (1975–76) and fifth seasons (1976–77), Oilers and Bulls, 34 and 41 goals
74 – *Anders Lee, fourth (2016–17) and fifth (2017–18) seasons, Islanders, 34 and 40 goals
72 – Mike Antonovich, fifth and sixth seasons (1976–78), Oilers, Whalers and Fighting Saints, 40 and 32 goals
68 – Jason Blake, sixth and seventh seasons (2005–7), Islanders, 28 and 40 goals
67 – Dave Christian, fourth and fifth seasons (1984–86), Capitals, 26 and 41 goals
59 – *T.J. Oshie, eighth and ninth seasons (first two with Capitals) (2015–17), 26 and 33 goals
55 – David Backes, fifth and sixth seasons (2010–12), Blues, 31 and 24 goals
53 – Mark Parrish, third and fourth seasons (2001–3), Islanders, 30 and 23 goals
52 – Aaron Broten, sixth and seventh seasons (1986–88), Devils, 26 and 26 goals
52 – Paul Holmgren, third and fourth seasons (1979–81), Flyers, 30 and 22 goals

Points, Best Three Consecutive Seasons
264 – Neal Broten, first 3 full seasons in NHL, North Stars (1981–84), 98, 77, 89
259 – Phil Housley, first 3 seasons, Jets (1990–93), 76, 86, 97
256 – *Blake Wheeler, Jets (2016–19), 74, 91, 91
241 – *Zach Parise, Devils (2007–10), 65, 94, 82
233 – Mark Pavelich, Rangers (1981–84), 76, 75, 82
213 – Dave Christian, Capitals (1983–86), 81, 69, 83
198 – Reed Larson, Red Wings (1982–85), 74, 62, 62
197 – Tim Sheehy, Oilers, Bulls, Whalers (1974–77), 62, 65, 70

Most Goals, Four Consecutive Seasons
146 – *Zach Parise, 31, 32, 45, 38 goals
143 – Tim Sheehy, 29, 39, 34, 41 goals
135 – Dave Christian, 41, 23, 37, 34 goals
121 – Mike Antonovich, 24, 25, 40, 32 goals
117 – Neal Broten, 38, 32, 28, 19 goals

115 – Jason Blake, 25, 22, 28, 40 goals
106 – *Blake Wheeler, 28, 26, 26, 26 goals
102 – *T.J. Oshie, 26, 33, 18, 25 goals

Most Career Power Play Points
612 – Phil Housley (South St. Paul)
291 – Neal Broten (Roseau)
273 – Reed Larson (Mpls. Roosevelt)
254 – Dave Christian (Warroad)
246 – *Zach Parise (Shattuck–St. Mary's)
222 – *Blake Wheeler (Breck)
202 – Dustin Byfuglein (Roseau)
185 – *T.J. Oshie (Warroad)
185 – Jamie Langenbrenner (Cloquet)
178 – Matt Cullen (Moorhead)

Career Power Play Goals
129 – Phil Housley (South St. Paul)
120 – *Zach Parise (Shattuck-St. Mary's)
102 – Dave Christian (Warroad)
88 – Reed Larson (Mpls. Roosevelt)
80 – *T.J. Oshie (Warroad)
67 – Neal Broten (Roseau)
67 – Jamie Langenbrenner (Cloquet)

Most Power Play Points in a Season
57 – Phil Housley (South St. Paul), 1992–93, Jets
40 – *Blake Wheeler (Breck), 2017–18, Jets
38 – Neal Broten (Roseau), 1985–86, North Stars
35 – Dave Christian (Warroad), 1985–86, Capitals
31 – Reed Larson (Mpls. Roosevelt), 1978–79, Red Wings
30 – *Zach Parise (Shattuck–St. Mary's), 2008–9, Devils

Most Power Play Goals in a Season
14 – *Anders Lee (Edina), 2017–18, Islanders
14 – *Zach Parise (Shattuck–St. Mary's), 2008–9, Devils and 2013–14, Wild
14 – Jason Blake (Moorhead), 2006–7, Islanders
14 – Scott Bjugstad (Irondale), 1985–86, North Stars
13 – Phil Housley (South St. Paul), 1983–84, Sabres

12 – Jamie Langenbrenner (Cloquet), 2007–8, Devils
12 – Jason Blake (Moorhead), 2005–6, Islanders
11 – Reed Larson (Mpls. Roosevelt), 1985–6, Red Wings
11 – *T.J. Oshie (Warroad), 2015–16, Capitals
10 – David Backes (Spring Lake Park), 2013–14, Blues and 2014–15, Blues
10 – Joel Otto (Elk River), 1988–89, Flames
10 – *Brock Nelson (Warroad), 2014–15, Islanders

Most Two-Goal Scorers on the Same Team in the Same Season
(numbers are goals and rank on the team)
2008–9 New Jersey Devils
45, 1 – Zach Parise
29, 3 – Jamie Langenbrenner
74 Total

1985–86 Minnesota North Stars
43, 2 – Scott Bjugstad
29, 4 – Neal Broten
72 Total

1981–82 Minnesota North Stars
38, 3 – Neal Broten
26, 5 – Steve Christoff
64 Total

1982–83 New York Rangers
37, 1 – Mark Pavelich
22, 5 – Rob McClanahan
59 Total

2009–10 New Jersey Devils
38, 1 – Zach Parise
19, 4 – Jame Langenbrenner
57 Total

1972–73 Minnesota Fighting Saints
36, 2 – Bill Klatt
20, 3 – Mike Antonovich
56 Total

2006–7 New Jersey Devils
31, 1–Zach Parise
23, 4–Jamie Langenbrenner
54 Total

2005–6 New York Islanders
28, 2–Jason Blake
24, 3–Mark Parrish
52 Total

1973–74 New England Whalers
29, 2–Tim Sheehy (tied)
21, 6–Tommy Williams
50 Total

2013–15 Winnipeg Jets
28, 1–Blake Wheeler
20, 4–Dustin Byfuglein
48 Total

2013–14 St. Louis Blues
27, 1–David Backes (57 points, third)
21, 4–T.J. Oshie (60 point, second)
48 Total

2002–3 New York Islanders
25, 2–Jason Blake (55 points, second)
23, 3–Mark Parrish (45 points, third)
48 Total

1980–81 Philadelphia Flyers
24, 5–Tom Gorence
22, 6–Paul Holmgren
46 Total

TABLE 9
CAREER PLAYOFF GAMES WITH TOTAL PLAYOFF GOALS, ASSISTS AND POINTS
*Active Player

162	*Ryan McDonagh (Cretin Derham, 2007)	11	48	59
146	Jamie Langenbrenner (Cloquet, 1993)	34	53	87
140	Matt Niskanen (Virgina, 2005)	6	36	42
135	Neal Broten (Roseau, 1978)	35	63	98
132	Matt Cullen (Moorhead, 1995)	19	39	58
127	Shjon Podein (Rochester John Marshall, 1986)	14	13	27
122	Paul Martin (Elk River, 2000)	6	40	46
122	Joel Otto (Elk River, 1981)	27	46	73
121	*Nick Leddy (Eden Prairie)	7	26	33
115	Mike Ramsey (Mpls. Roosevelt-1978)	8	29	37
110	Dave Langevin (Hill-Murray-1972)	4	21	25
108	Bret Hedican (North St. Paul)	4	44	46
106	*Derek Stepan (Shattuck–St. Mary's)	20	34	54
105	*Zach Parise (Shattuck–St. Mary's)	37	43	80
102	Dave Christian (Warroad)	32	25	57
96	*T.J. Oshie (Warroad-2003)	28	33	61
85	Phil Housley (South St. Paul)	13	43	56
83	Patrick Eaves (Shattuck–St. Mary's)	11	12	23
82	David Backes (Spring Lake Park)	17	22	39
82	Paul Holmgren (St. Paul Harding)	19	32	51
68	*Nate Schmidt (St. Cloud Cathedral)	6	12	25
67	*Brock Nelson (Warroad)	23	18	41

66	Dustin Byfuglein (Roseau-2003)	21	29	50
60	*Blake Wheeler (Breck)	8	31	39
57	Tom Kurvers (Bloomington Jefferson)	8	22	30
51	*Jake Guentzel (Hill-Murray)	26	22	48
45	Ryan Carter (White Bear Lake)	7	5	12

TABLE 10
CAREER PLAYOFF GOALS

37	*Zach Parise (Shattuck–St. Mary's, 2003)
35	Neal Broten (Roseau, 1978)
34	Jamie Langenbrenner (Cloquet, 1993)
32	Dave Christian (Warroad, 1977)
28	*T.J. Oshie (Warroad, 2005)
21	Dustin Byfuglein (Roseau, 2003)

TABLE 11
CAREER PLAYOFF POINTS

98	Neal Broten (Roseau, 1978)
87	Jamie Langenbrenner (Cloquet, 1993)
*80	*Zach Parise (Shattuck–St. Mary's, 2003)
73	Joel Otto (Elk River, 1981)
61	*T.J. Oshie (Warroad, 2005)
58	Matt Cullen (Moorhead, 1995)
57	Dave Christian (Warroad, 1977)
56	Phil Housley (South St. Paul, 1982)

Most Playoff Points in One Stanley Cup Playoffs
*Stanley Cup Playoffs
In close-checking, high-intensity, high-speed playoffs, these players rose to the top with a tremendous offensive playoffs, leading their teams sometimes to the Stanley Cup.

23 – Tim Sheehy, 1973, Whalers* (15 games)
22 – Neal Broten, 1991, North Stars
21 – Jake Guentzel-Twice-2017* & 2018-Penguins (2018 in 12 games)
21 – T.J. Oshie, 2018, Capitals*
21 – Blake Wheeler, 2018, Jets
20 – Paul Holmgren, 1980, Flyers
19 – Neal Broten, 1995, Devils*
18 – Jamie Langenbrenner, 2003, Devils* (tied for most in playoffs)
17 – Mike Antonovich, 1978, Whalers (led the playoffs)
17 – Matt Cullen, 2006, Hurricanes*
17 – Ryan McDonagh, 2014, Rangers
16 – Dustin Byfuglien, 2010, Blackhawks* and 2018, Jets
16 – Steve Christoff, 1981, North Stars
16 – Aaron Broten, 1988, Devils
15 – Tom Kurvers, 1988, Devils
15 – Zach Parise, 2012, Devils
15 – Derek Stepan, 2014, Rangers

Most Playoff Goals in One Stanley Cup Playoffs
* = Stanley Cup Championship Playoffs.

13 – Jake Guentzel, 2017, Penguins* (led the playoffs)
11 – Jamie Langenbrenner, 2003, Devils* (led the playoffs)
11 – Dustin Byfuglien, 2010, Blackhawks*
10 – Mike Antonovich, 1978, Whalers (led the playoffs)
10 – Paul Holmgren, 1980, Flyers
10 – Jamie Langenbrenner, 1999, Stars*
9 – Neal Broten, 1991, North Stars
9 – Tim Sheehy, 197, Whalers*
9 – Brock Nelson, 2020, Islanders
8 – T.J. Oshie, 2018, Capitals*
8 – Dave Christian, 1991, Bruins
8 – Steve Christoff, 1980 and 1981, North Stars
8–Zach Parise, 2012, Devils

TABLE 12
STANLEY CUP CHAMPIONSHIPS

4	David Langevin (Hill-Murray)	Islanders 1980, 1981, 1982, 1983
3	Bill Nyrop (Edina)	Canadiens 1976, 1977, 1978
3	Matt Cullen (Moorhead)	Hurricanes 2006; Penguins 2016, 2017
2	Bob Johnson (Mpls. Central)	Penguins 1991, 1992 (as coach)
2	Jamie Langenbrenner (Cloquet)	Stars 1999; Devils 2003
2	Frank Brimsek (Eveleth)	Bruins 1939, 1941
2	Ryan McDonagh (Cretin-Derham)	Lightning 2020, 2021
2	Elwyn "Doc" Romnes (St. Paul Mechanic Arts)	Blackhawks 1934, 1938
1	Cully Dahlstrom (Mpls. South)	Blackhawks 1938
1	Mike Karakas (Eveleth)	Blackhawks 1938
1	T.J. Oshie (Warroad)	Capitals 2018
1	Nick Leddy (Eden Prairie)	Blackhawks 2012
1	Dustin Byfuglein (Roseau)	Blackhawks 2012
1	Tom Kurvers (Bloomington Jefferson)	Canadiens 1986
1	Jake Guentzel (Hill-Murray)	Penguins 2017
1	Neal Broten (Roseau)	Devils 1995
1	Joel Otto (Elk River)	Flames 1989
1	Bret Hedican (North St. Paul)	Hurricanes 2006
1	Sean Hill (Duluth East)	Canadiens 1993
1	Ben Clymer (Bloomington Jefferson)	Lightning 2004

1	Ryan Carter (White Bear Lake)	Ducks 2007
1	Shjon Podein (Rochester John Marshall)	Avalanche 2001
1	Dave Maley (Edina)	Canadiens 1986
1	Chris McAlpine (Roseville)	Devils 1995
1	Tom Chorske (Mpls. Southwest)	Devils 1995
1	Mike Peluso (Hibbing)	Devils 1995
1	Mike Polich (Hibbing)	Canadiens 1978
1	Aaron Ness (Roseau)	Capitals 2018
1	Todd Richards (Assistant Coach)	Lightning-2020

WHA AVCO Cup Championship

1 Tommy Williams (Duluth Central) Whalers, 1973
1 Tim Sheehy (International Falls) Whalers, 1973

TABLE 13
HOCKEY HALL OF FAME

Phil Housley (South St. Paul High School)	Defense	1982–2003, inducted 2015
Frank Brimsek (Eveleth High School)	Goalie	1938–50, inducted 1966
Moose Goheen (White Bear Lake High School)	Left-wing	1915–22, inducted 1952
Walter Bush (Builder)		inducted 2000
Herb Brooks (St. Paul Johnson High School 1955) (Builder)		inducted 2006

TABLE 14
BEST SEASON PLUS-MINUS*

56	Bill Nyrop	1977–78 Canadiens
42	Bill Nyrop	1976–77 Canadiens
40	Dave Langevin	1980–81 Islanders
38	Ryan McDonagh	2018–19 Lightning
36	Blake Wheeler	2008–9 Bruins
35	Paul Holmgren	1979–80 Flyers
33	Matt Niskanen	2013–14 Penguins
32	David Backes	2010–11 Blues
30	Mike Ramsey	1984–85 Sabres
30	Zach Parise	2008–9 Devils
30	Don Jackson	1984–85 Oilers
28	T.J. Oshie	2016–17 Capitals

*Plus-minus record is of questionable value, certainly a lower value than other records. Some attribute it to luck and to the play of the other five players on the ice for each shift. Nevertheless in the official NHL records for every nongoalie NHL player, one of the five stats is plus-minus for each season and for their career. For fun, these season plus-minus records show that these players were part of a team that had a good to really good year.

Career: Plus/Minus
205 – Mike Ramsey in 19 seasons
198 – *Ryan McDonagh in 13 seasons
133 – Bill Nyrop in 5 seasons
119 – *T.J. Oshie in 14 seasons
112 – Matt Niskanen in 14 seasons
103 – Dave Langevin in 9 seasons

TABLE 15
TWELVE BLUE LINERS
Career Statistics in Order of Games Played

Player (Years Active)	Team (Seasons Played)	Games (Playoff Games)	
Phil Housley (1982–2003) 20 Seasons	Sabres (8) Jets (3) Flames (5) Capitals (2)	1,495 (85)	
Mike Ramsey (1980–97) 18 Seasons	Sabres (14) Penguins (1) Red Wings (3)	1,070 (115)	
Reed Larson (1977–90) 13 Seasons	Red Wings (10) Bruins (3) Oilers (1) Islanders (1) North Stars (1)	904 (32)	
Jim Johnson (1985–98) 13 Seasons	Penguins (5) North Stars—Stars—Capitals—Coyotes	829 (51)	

APPENDIX

Goals	Assists	Points	All Star Selections	Hall of Fame Induction	Stanley Cup Titles
338	894	1,232	7: 1984, 1989, 1990, 1991, 1992, 1993, 2000	2015	0
79	266	345	4: 1982, 1983, 1985, 1986	-	0
222	463	685	4: 1978, 1980, 1981, 1983	0	0
29	166	195	-	0	0

Player (Years Active)	Team (Seasons Played)	Games (Playoff Games)	
Dave Langevin (1976–87) 11 Seasons	Oilers (3) Islanders (6) North Stars–Kings (1)	729 (110)	
Tom Kurvers (1984–95) 10 Seasons	Caanadians (2) Sabres (1) Devils (2) Maple Leafs (2) Islanders (3)	659 (57)	
Jim Korn (1979–90) 9 Seasons	Red Wings (3) Maple Leafs (3) Sabres (1) Devils (3)	597 (16)	
Chris Dahlquist (1985–97) 10 Seasons	Pentuins (6) North Stars (2) Flames (2) Senators (2)	532 (39)	
Russ Anderson (1976–85) 8 Seasons	Penguins (6) Whalers (2) Kings (2)	519 (10)	
Bob Paradise (1971–79) 8 Seasons	North Stars (1) Flames (2) Penguins (5) Capitals (2)	368 (12)	
Don Jackson (1977–87) 9 Seasons	North Stars (4) Oilers (5) Rangers (1)	315 (53)	
Bill Nyrop (1976–78+) 4 Seasons	Canadians (3) North Stars (1)	207 (35)	

Goals	Assists	Points	All Star Selections	Hall of Fame Induction	Stanley Cup Titles
31	166	197	2: 1979, 1983	0	4: Islanders 1980, 1981, 1982, 1983.
93	328	421	0	0	1: Canadiens 1986
66	122	188	0	0	0
19	71	90	0	0	0
22	99	121	0	0	0
8	54	62	0	0	0
16	52	68	0	0	2: Oilers 1984, 1985
12	51	63	0	0	3: Canadiens 1976,1977, 1978

TABLE 16
FOUR FORWARDS AND ONE DEFENSEMAN FROM TWO HOCKEY TOWNS
Career Statistics in Order of Games Played

Player Name (Years Active)	Team (No. of Seasons Played)	Games (Playoff Games)	
Neal Broten (1981–99) 18 Seasons	North Stars (13) Stars (2) Devils (2) Kings/ Stars (1)	1,098 (135)	
Dave Christian (1980–96) 15 Seasons	Jets (4) Capitals (7) Bruins (1) Blues (1) Blackhawks (2)	1,009 (102)	
Aaron Broten (1981–92) 12 Seasons	Rockies (2) Devils (8) North Stars (1) Nordiques (1) Maple Leafs (1) Jets (1)	748 (32)	
Alan Hangsleben (1974–82) 10 Seasons	Whalers (6) Capitals (3) Kings (1)	519 (47)	
Henry Boucha (1972–77) 6 Seasons	Red Wings (3) North Stars (1) Fighting Saints (1) Scouts (1) Rockies (1)	283 (14)	

Goals	Assists	Points	All Star Selections	Hall of Fame Year of Induction	Stanley Cup Titles
289	634	923	1983, 1986	0	1: Devils 1995
340	423	775	0	0	0
186	329	515	0	0	0
57	121	178	0	0	0
68	69	137	0	0	0

TABLE 17
GRITTY PLAYERS
Career Statistics in Order of Games Played

Player (Years Active)	Team (No. of Seasons Played)	Games (Playoff Games)	
Joel Otto (1984–98) 14 Seasons	Flames (11) Flyers (3)	943 (122)	
Mike Antonovich (1972–84) 12 Seasons	Fighting Saints (4) North Stars (2) Oilers (1) Whalers (3) Devils (2)	575 (58)	
Paul Holmgren (1975–85) 11 Seasons	Fighting Saints (1) Flyers (9) North Stars (2)	527 (82)	
Jack Carlson (1974–87) 11 Seasons	Fighting Saints (3) Oilers (1) Whalers (3) North Stars (4) Blues (2)	527 (82)	
Warren Miller (1975–83) 8 Seasons	Cowboys (2) Oilers (1) Nordiques (1) Whalers (4) Rangers (1)	500 (37)	
Dean Talafous (1974–82) 8 Seasons	Flames (1) North Stars (3) Rangers (4)	497 (21)	
Tim Sheehy (1972–80) 8 Seasons	Oilers (3) Bulls (2) Red Wings (1) Whalers (5)	460 (39)	
Steve Jensen (1975–82) 7 Seasons	North Stars (3) Kings (4)	438 (12)	
Tom Younghans (1976–82) 8 Seasons	North Stars (7) Rangers (8)	429 (24)	
Jon Casey (1984–98) 13 Seasons	North Stars (8) Bruins (1) Blues (4)	425	
Gary Sargent (1975–83) 8 Seasons	Kings (3) North Stars (5)	402(20)	

Goals	Assists	Points	All Star Selections	Hall of Fame Year of Induction	Stanley Cup Titles
195	313	508	0	0	1: Flames 1989
192	203	395	1:1978	0	0
144	179	323	1: 1981	0	0
66	66	132	0	0	0
105	133	238	0	0	0
104	154	258	0	0	0
180	174	354	0	0	1: WHA AVCO Cup New England Whalers 1973
113	107	220	0	0	0
44	41	85	0	0	0
170 Wins	157 Losses	55 Ties	1: 1993	0	0
61	161	222	1: 1980	0	0

Table 18

Pre–Golden Era Players

Career Statistics in Order of Games Played

Player (Years Active)	Team (No. of Seasons Played)	Games (Playoff Games)	
Tommy Williams (1961–75) 13 Seasons	Bruins (8) North Stars (2) Golden Seals (2) Whalers (2)	803 (29)	
Frank Brimsek (1939–50) 10 Seasons	Bruins (10)	514	
Elwyn "Doc" Romnes (1930–40) 10 Seasons	Blackhawks (9) Maple Leafs (1)	360	
Mike Karakas (1935–46) 8 Seasons	Blackhawks (8)	336	
Cully Dahlstrom (1937–45) 8 Seasons	Blackhawks (8)	342	
John Mariucci (1940–52) 8 Seasons	Blackhawks (8)	223	

Goals	Assists	Career Points	All Star Selections	Hall of Fame Year of Induction	Stanley Cup Titles
192	357	519	0	0	1: WHA AVCO Cup, New England Whalers 1973
252 Wins	182 Losses	80 Ties	8: 1939, 1940, 1941, 1942, 1943, 1946, 1947, 1948	***1952	2: Bruins 1939, 1941
67	137	204	0	0	2: Blackhawks 1934, 1938
114 Wins	169 Losses	53 Ties	1: 1945	0	1: Blackhawks 1938
88	118	206	0	0	1: Blackhawks 1938
11	34	45	0	0	0

TABLE 19
POST–GOLDEN ERA PLAYERS
Career Statistics in Order of Games Played

Player (Years Active)	Team (No. of Seasons Played)	Games (Playoff Games)	
Bret Hedican (1991–2009) 17 Seasons	Blues (3) Canucks (6) Panthers (4) Hurricanes (6) Devils (1)	1,019 (108)	
Paul Ranheim (1988–2003) 17 Seasons	Flames (6) Whalers (4) Hurricanes (3) Flyers (3) Coyotes (1)	1,013 (36)	
Sean Hill (1991–2009) 15 Seasons	Canadians (3) Ducks (1) Senators (4) Hurricanes (6) Blues (2) Panthers (1) Islanders (1) Wild (1)	870 (55)	
Trent Klatt (1992–2004) 12 Seasons	North Stars (2) Stars (2) Flyers (2) Canucks (5) Kings (1)	782 (74)	
Shjon Podein (1994–2006) 11 Seasons	Oilers (1) Flyers (5) Avalanche (3) Blues (2)	699 (127)	
Tom Chorske (1989–2001) 11 Seasons	Canadians (2) Devils (4) Senators (2) Islanders (2) Capitals (1) Flames (1) Penguins (1)	596 (50)	
Damian Rhodes (1990–2002) 11 Seasons	Maple Leafs (4) Senators (4) Flames (3)	309 (13) Goalie	

Goals	Assists	Points	All Star Selections	Hall of Fame Year of Induction	Stanley Cup Titles
55	239	294	0	0	1: Hurricanes 2006
161	199	360	0	0	0
62	236	298	0	0	1: Canadiens 1993
143	200	343	0	0	0
100	106	206	0	9	0
115	122	237	0	0	1: Devils 1995
99 Wins	140 Losses	48 Ties			

TABLE 20
Minnesota Forwards in the NHL Draft
Career Statistics in Order of Games Played

Player (Years Active)	Team (No. of Seasons Played)	Games (Playoff Games)	
Matt Cullen (1997–2019) 21 Seasons	Ducks (6) Panthers (2) Hurricanes (4) Rangers (1) Wild (4) Predators (2) Penguins (3) Senators (1)	1,516 (132)	
Jamie Langenbrenner (1995–2013) 17 Seasons	Stars (8) Devils (9) Stars (1) Blues (2)	1,109 (146)	
Jason Blake (1999–2012) 12 Seasons	Kings (3) Islanders (6) Maple Leafs (3) Ducks (2)	871 (30)	
Mark Parrish (1998–2011) 12 Seasons	Panthers (2) Islanders (5) Kings (1) Wild (2) Stars (1) Lightning (1) Sabres (1)	732 (27)	
Matt Hendricks (2008–2019) 10 Seasons	Rockies (2) Capitals (3) Predators (1) Oilers (4) Jets (2) Wild (1)	607 (38)	
Craig Johnson (1994–2004) 9 Seasons	Blues (2) Kings (7) Ducks (1) Leafs (91) Capitals (1)	557 (16)	
Erik Rasmussen (1997–2009) 9 Seasons	Sabres (5) Kings (1) Devils (3)	545 (52)	
Darby Hendrickson (1993–2004) 10 Seasons	Maple Leafs (6) Islanders (1) Canucks (2) Wild (4) Avalanche (1)	518 (25)	

Goals	Assists	Career Points	All Star Selections	Hall of Fame Year of Induction	Stanley Cup Titles
266	465	731	0	0	
243	420	663	0	0	2: Stars1999, Devils 2003
213	273	486	2007	0	0
216	171	387	2002	0	0
54	62	116	0	0	0
75	98	173	0	0	0
52	76	128	0	0	0
65	64	129	0	0	0

TABLE 21
MINNESOTA DEFENSEMEN IN THE NHL DRAFT

Career Statistics in Order of Games Played

Player (Years Active)	Team (No. of Seasons Played)	Games (Playoff Games)	
Paul Martin (2003–18) 14 Seasons	Devils (6) Penguins (5) Sharks (3)	870 (122)	
Jordan Leopold (2002–015) 13 Seasons	Flames (4) Avalanche (3) Panthers (1) Penguins (1) Sabres (2) Blues (3)	695 (80)	
Mark Stuart (2005–17) 12 Seasons	Bruins (6) Flames/Jets (7)	673 (26)	
Tom Gilbert (2006–16) 10 Seasons	Oilers (6) Wild (2) Panthers (1) Canadians (2) Kings (1)	655 (17)	
Keith Ballard (2004–15) 10 Seasons	Coyotes (3) Panthers (2) Canucks (3) Wild (2)	604 (17)	

Goals	Assists	Points	All Star Selections	Hall of Fame Year of Induction	Stanley Cup Titles
50	270	320	0	0	0
67	147	214	0	0	0
26	67	93	0	0	0
45	178	223	0	0	0
38	137	175	0	0	0

TABLE 22

GRAND SEVEN YEARS. MINNESOTA TALENT IN THE NHL DRAFT (2002–9)

Career Statistics in Order of Games Played

Player (Years Active)	Team (No. of Seasons Played)	Games (Playoff Games)	
Zach Parise (2005–Present) 15-plus Seasons	Islanders (1) Devils (7) Wild (9)	1,094 (105)	
Blake Wheeler (2008–Present) 12-plus Seasons	Bruins (2) Flames (1) Jets (10)	981 (52)	
David Backes (2006–Present) 14-plus Seasons	Blues (10) Bruins (2) Ducks (2)	965 (82)	
Matt Niskanen (2007–20) 12 Seasons	Stars (4) Penguins (4) Capitals (5) Islanders (1)	949 (140)	
Alex Goligoski (2007–Present) 13 Seasons	Penguins (4) Stars (6) Coyotes (5) Wild (1)	924 (43)	
Dustin Byfuglien (2007–20) 12 Seasons.	Blackhawks (5) Flames (1) Jets (8).	869 (66)	
T.J. Oshie (2008–Present) 12+ Seasons	Blues (7) Capitals (6)	856 (96)	
Kyle Okposo (2008–Present) 12+ Seasons	Islanders (9) Sabres (5)	835 (24)	
Erik Johnson (2007–Present) 13 Seasons	Blues (3) Avalanche (11)	780 (28)	
Nick Leddy (2007–Present) 13 Seasons	Blackhawks (4) Islanders (7).	776 (110)	
Justin Braun (2010–21) 11 Seasons	Sharks (9) Flyers (2)	772 (100)	
Derek Stepan (2010–Present) 12+ Seasons	Rangers (7) Coyotes (3) Senators (1)	759 (106)	
Ryan McDonagh (2010–Present) 12 Seasons	Rangers (8) Lightning (4)	712 (162)	

Goals	Assists	Points	All Star Selections	Hall of Fame Year of Induction	Stanley Cup Titles
395	425	820	2009	0	0
279	528	807	2018, 2019	0	0
248	313	561	2011	0	0
72	284	356	0	0	1: Capitals 2018
83	346	429	0	0	0
177	340	525	2011, 2012, 2015, 2016	0	1: Blackhawks 2012
260	350	610	2020	0	1: Capitals 2018
196	321	519	2017	0	0
80	224	302	0	0	0
65	271	336	0	0	1: Blackhawks 2012
28	151	179	0	0	0
165	317	485	0	0	0
67	244	373	2016, 2017	0	2: Lightning 2020, 2021

Player (Years Active)	Team (No. of Seasons Played)	Games (Playoff Games)	
Justin Faulk (2011–Present) 10 Seasons	Hurricanes (8) Blues (2)	684 (26)	
Jake Gardiner (2011–Present) 10 Seasons	Maple Leafs (8) Hurricanes (2)	643 (33)	
Patrick Eaves (2005–2019) 15 Seasons	Senators (3) Hurricanes (2) Red Wings (5) Stars (2) Ducks (3)	633 (83)	
Brock Nelson (2013–Present) 8 Seasons	Islanders (8)	604 (67)	
Anders Lee (2012–Present) 9 Seasons	Islanders (9)	520 (35)	

Goals	Assists	Points	All Star Selections	Hall of Fame Year of Induction	Stanley Cup Titles
97	202	299	2016, 2016, 2017	0	0
49	228	277	0	0	0
132	110	242	0	0	0
168	160	328	0	0	0
184	136	320	0	0	0

NOTES

1. Ken Dryden, *Scotty: A Hockey Life Like No Other* (Toronto: McClelland & Stewart, 2019), 222.
2. Vintage Minnesota Hockey, "Arenas," www.vintagemnhockey.com.
3. Ibid., "State Tournament."
4. Ibid.
5. United States Census Bureau, www.census.gov.
6. Metronet, "Corporate Archivist, General Mills," www.metrolibraries.net.
7. Douglas Brinkley, *Wilderness Warrior: Theodore Roosevelt and the Crusade for America* (New York: Harper Collins, 1999), 14.
8. United States Census Bureau.
9. Ibid.
10. Ibid.
11. Vintage Minnesota Hockey, "MCHA, Coach Ikola."
12. Hill-Murray School, "Hockey," www.hill-murray.org.
13. Ibid.
14. Greatest Hockey Legends, January 17, 2007. www.greatesthockeylegends.com.
15. Vintage Minnesota Hockey, "MCHA, Coach Freeburg."
16. Ibid.
17. Ibid., "MCHA, Coach Woog."
18. Ibid., "MCHA, Coach Saterdalen."
19. Ibid., "MCHA, Coach Staples."

20. National Hockey League, "Coaching Records," www.nhl.com.
21. Leith Dunick, "Former NHLer Rudy Migay Dies at 87," TBNewsWatch.com, January 17, 2016, www.tbnewswatch.com.
22. Dryden, *Scotty*, 222.
23. Ibid., 203.
24. Ibid., 202.
25. Ibid.
26. Ibid.
27. National Hockey League, www.nhl.com.
28. NHL.com.
29. Dryden, *Scotty*, 370.
30. NHL.com.
31. NHL.com.
32. NHL.com.
33. "Vintage MN Hockey".
34. Dryden, *Scotty*, 371.
35. Ibid., 323.
36. Minnesota State High School League, www.mshsl.org.
37. United States High School Hockey, www.ushsho.com.
38. NCAA, "Men's Ice Hockey, Division I," www.ncaa.com/sports/icehockey-men/d1.
39. NHL.com.
40. NHL.com.
41. NHL.com.

ABOUT THE AUTHOR

Jeff Olson has coached hockey at a number of levels. He's coached youth hockey, pee wee and bantam teams; high school as an assistant coach at West St. Paul Sibley, New Ulm and Litchfield; and at the small college level as an assistant at Hamline University. He also officiated youth and adult hockey and served as an organizer of the Gunderson Lake Conference Hockey Awards Scholarship Golf Classic for a number of years.

Jeff grew up in Mendota Heights with legendary hockey figures everywhere. He played high school hockey at Breck School for Dr. Jack Blatherwick. In his youth, Jeff attended Ken Yackel Hockey School with Lou Nanne as a counselor.

Jeff currently serves as an arbitrator. He served as a referee, part time, at Ramsey County Conciliation Court for over ten years and worked as a trial attorney for over thirty-six years. He has served in a number of capacities with a number of Minnesota nonprofits and charities, including: board chair of STEP Academy, a Minnesota charter school; president of Parks & Trails Council of Minnesota; president of Fort Snelling State Park Association; president of Eden Prairie Rotary A.M. Club; commissioner of Three Rivers Park District; and president of All Saints Lutheran Church of Minnetonka.

Jeff and his wife, Sue, live in Eden Prairie, Minnesota. They share a passion for reading, great food, theater, music, hiking, biking, golfing, visiting parks and traveling. They plan to visit all the wonderful state parks of Minnesota and every Minnesota hockey arena.

Visit us at
www.historypress.com
···